AEI Legislative Analyses
*Balanced analyses of current proposals before the Congress, prepared with the help of specialists in law, economics, and government*

# Recent Proposals to Restrict Conglomerate Mergers

1981

97th Congress
1st Session



American Enterprise Institute
for Public Policy Research
*Washington and London*

ISBN 0-8447-0240-4
Legislative Analysis No. 25, 97th Congress
July 1981

# CONTENTS

# 1
# INTRODUCTION

Conglomerate mergers, which join firms that do not stand in a buyer-seller relationship and do not compete with one another in the same market, have increased significantly in the last two decades. This increase has spurred demands in some quarters for the adoption of new antimerger legislation or other measures to prevent the concentration of business in the hands of fewer and fewer organizations. Recent antimerger proposals are not limited in their terms to conglomerate mergers but would cover any merger involving firms above a specified size. The Sherman Antitrust Act and the Clayton Antitrust Act, however, already deal with horizontal mergers (those involving firms that produce the same product and compete with one another) and vertical mergers (those joining firms that stand in a buyer-seller relation to each other). Price fixing and other anticompetitive conduct are already illegal under existing law. Thus, the principal purpose of recent legislative proposals is to facilitate challenging the merger of firms in unrelated lines of business and the merger of firms that operate in different geographical markets.

Advocates of new restrictions on conglomerate mergers do not limit their arguments to the usual antitrust concerns for the economic consequences of mergers or to market efficiency. Rather, they emphasize the asserted need to restrict conglomerate mergers for political and social reasons.

Thus, the principal recent antimerger proposals do not call for marginal changes in existing law. Rather, they recommend a fundamental shift in the direction of antimerger law. Critics refer to these proposals as "no-fault" antimerger plans that attack bigness for itself.

This analysis will examine the provisions of recent proposals to restrict conglomerate mergers and canvass the reasons for and against their adoption.

# 2

## Background

Mergers historically have come in waves, triggered largely by general economic conditions, but affected also by patterns of antitrust enforcement. Not surprisingly, antitrust law relating to mergers has developed largely in response to the trends in merger activity.

### History of Mergers and Development of Related Antitrust Law

The first great wave of merger activity began in 1879, with the formation of the Standard Oil Trust, and continued until 1904. During that period the economy was characterized by available capital and rapid industrialization. As transportation and communications improved, geographic markets expanded and firms that previously had faced little competition found themselves battling distant rivals. The new competition provided an incentive to merge, and several large industrial combinations were assembled before 1893. After that, merger activity slowed because of an economic depression and uncertainty created by the passage of the Sherman Act in 1890. It resumed, however, in 1895 when a Supreme Court decision, now regarded as aberrant, suggested that 98 percent of an industry's capacity could be consolidated without violating the Sherman Act. The period between 1897 and 1904 saw an "avalanche of horizontal merger activity."[1] This activity affected more than 15 percent of all manufacturing plants and employees.[2] By 1904, productive capacity in basic industry after basic industry had come under the domination of a single firm. Of ninety-two large consolidations, seventy-eight resulted in firms with market shares of at least 50 percent, and twenty-six in firms with 80 percent.[3]

Merger activity declined sharply in 1904, in the face of a severe depression and the Supreme Court's decision in *Northern Securities Company* v. *United States*.[4] That decision concluded that mergers resulting in market dominance could be attacked under the Sherman Act. More significantly, the legal community of the era focused upon Justice John M. Harlan's view that any arrangement eliminating competition between two previously competing corporations violated the Sherman Act, even though the view failed to command a majority of the Court.[5]

The Court ultimately adopted a less sweeping stand in the oil and tobacco cases of 1911, when it interpreted the Sherman Act to prohibit only unreasonable restraints.[6] Both the oil and tobacco consolidations were held to violate the Sherman Act, but only because they were undue restraints transcending the act's lawful bounds. The enunciation of what has become known as the "rule of reason" was seen by some as essentially the repeal of the Sherman Act, and they pressed for new legislation to rejuvenate the weakened antitrust law. During "the election campaign of 1912, Taft, Roosevelt and Wilson and their parties, each in their own ways, committed themselves to legislation making the law more rigorous than the court had left it" with the rule of reason.[7]

Following Wilson's election, Congress in 1914 passed the Clayton Act and the Federal Trade Commission Act.[8] The latter established an "expert tribunal" to regulate economic activity. The former had several substantive provisions, the most relevant of which was an antimerger provision: Section 7 of the Clayton Act forbade any corporation engaged in commerce from acquiring the stock of another corporation also engaged in commerce, where the effect of the acquisition might be substantially to lessen competition between the two corporations or to tend to create a monopoly. The section was aimed at the most common device then used for consolidations—holding companies—and thus dealt only with acquisitions of stock.

Despite Section 7, a second great merger wave rode the stock market boom from 1920 to 1929. Now, however, mergers were achieved through asset acquisition, so as to avoid the terms of the Clayton Act. The Sherman Act remained available for challenging asset acquisitions, but its use was limited: courts were reluctant to find a merger by itself unlawful under the Sherman Act unless the merger was accompanied by abuse of the power acquired through the merger.

Although the second merger wave paralleled in volume its turn-of-the-century predecessor, the two had differences.[9] First, much of the activity during the 1920s involved electric and gas utilities. Because these firms typically were local monopolies before merger, their mergers worked only slight increases in monopoly power. Second, in the manufacturing sector, the mergers of the 1920s had far less impact on market structure than did the first wave. Multifirm consolidations were rarer, and resulting firms were seldom dominant. Nor did the mergers affect so wide a range of industries. Nearly half of the manufacturing-sector mergers involved food products, chemicals, and metals. Third, the activity of the 1920s was marked by a large number of vertical and diversification mergers. Previously, most mergers had been horizontal.

The Great Depression tolled the end of the second merger wave, and merger activity remained sparse throughout the 1930s. In the early 1940s, however, with the economy stimulated by World War II, a third wave began.

The legislative response was the passage in 1950 of the Celler-Kefauver Act, which amended Section 7 to increase its effectiveness.[10] The amendment applied Section 7 to all mergers, including asset acquisitions, and extended the section to cover any substantial reduction in competition generally, not just competition between the merging firms. The legislation was accompanied—and perhaps propelled through Congress—by considerable rhetoric about increases in aggregate concentration and by populist fears of undue increases in the number and power of large organizations.

The first case under the revised Clayton Act, *Brown Shoe Company* v. *United States,* adopted a restrictive stance toward merger activity.[11] Although the Court has since backed away in some details from the tough language of *Brown Shoe,* the language remains in the background and continues to influence analysis. As a result, public policy toward mergers involving direct competitive relationships has been quite strict. In fact, Section 7 has been interpreted to prohibit virtually all mergers involving substantial horizontal competitors.

The use of Section 7 to strike down horizontal and vertical mergers has inevitably channelled acquisition activity into the safer waters of conglomerate mergers—the acquisition of firms or assets in unrelated industries or markets. Since 1966, for example, roughly 80 percent of large acquisitions in manufacturing and mining have been conglomerate. That percentage has not changed in a marked trend over the period, although the volume of activity has fluctuated.[12]

The volume of merger activity—including conglomerate merger activity—has increased since 1972, although the volume has never again matched that of the peak year 1968. According to private statistics, the total purchase value of all reported corporate mergers and acquisitions increased from \$11.8 billion in 1975 to \$20.0 billion in 1976, to \$21.9 billion in 1977, and to \$34.2 billion in 1978. Among only those mergers in which the acquired firm was characterized as "large" by the Federal Trade Commission (FTC), because it had assets of \$10 million or more, volume declined to \$1.9 billion in 1972. Since then, however, it has been increasing: to \$4.7 billion in 1975, to \$6.3 billion in 1976, and to \$8.7 billion in 1977. Similarly, the number of mergers with a purchase value of more than \$100 million has increased in recent years, from fourteen such mergers in 1975 to thirty-nine in 1976, to forty-one in 1977, and to eighty in 1978.[13] Although continued inflation skews the numbers, it seems clear that acquisition activity continues at a fairly brisk pace today.

## Market Concentration and Economic Behavior

A basic premise of those who enforce the antitrust laws is that, when a market has few sellers, it may not be adequately competitive and consumers will have to pay higher prices than they would under competitive conditions or forgo purchases. The following elemental statement of the theory of the behavior of markets will establish the setting for the ongoing debate over antitrust policy, particularly as that debate relates to mergers.

Theorists claim that, in an industry with many sellers each of whom has only a small share of the market (sometimes referred to as an atomistic industry), each seller will normally assume that it cannot control pricing and will adjust its production volume to the level that is most profitable at the going market price. No seller can significantly affect the market by contracting or expanding production, and impersonal market forces will determine the ultimate price level. Industry production will be expanded and prices reduced, until the marginal cost of supplying a unit of production equals the price at which that unit will then sell in the market.[14]

In a monopoly market there is but one seller and, if consumers cannot readily substitute other products, the seller can restrict production and attempt to set prices that maximize profit. Of course, if the seller is aware that charging supracompetitive prices may induce others to enter the industry, it may engage in limit pricing by setting a "maximum entry-forestalling price" to maximize long-run, as distinguished from short-run, profits while excluding potential competitors from the market. If the seller does not engage in limit pricing and charges supracompetitive prices, others may be induced to enter the market. Then the monopolist will share the market with these new sellers. Prospective entrants may be discouraged by entry barriers such as the monopolist's exclusive control of certain necessary supplies or its ownership of key patents, or by their own inability to obtain the government's grant of a franchise to serve a particular market. Of course, if the barriers to entry are low rather than high, the monopolist's limit pricing level must be set low to discourage entry.

An industry with so few sellers that the actions of one seller will materially affect the price of the product involved and thus have a significant impact on the seller's competitors is referred to as an oligopoly. This kind of market power is most common in manufacturing but far less common in the other sectors of the economy that account for three-fourths of output and employment. Antimerger enforcement activity is focused primarily on firms in these concentrated industries.

Pricing behavior in oligopolistic industries lies somewhere between the extremes described for monopoly industries and for atomistic industries. Advocates of stronger antimerger laws contend that the major sellers in an oligopolistic industry can easily agree on production volume or on prices and, if any firm departs from the agreement, this will be easy to detect so its competitors can retaliate. Of course, such price-fixing can be prosecuted under current antitrust law and no new legislation is required to deal with these cases. Advocates of stronger antimerger laws believe, however, that sellers in some oligopolistic industries may have tacit understandings or engage in soft competition so that in fact a few sellers in a concentrated industry may exercise considerable discretionary control over prices and thus maximize their profits.

The effect on competition of an acquisition of a firm in a concentrated industry, or a merger with it, may be easy to discern when the merger is horizontal but much more difficult to establish if the merger is conglomerate. Antitrust plaintiffs have advanced a series of theories to develop court-made law to deal with mergers. These theories are discussed in the next section. Industry concentration, with its claimed concomitant effect on market behavior and pricing, is a precondition to the successful application of these theories to block conglomerate acquisitions and mergers under existing antitrust law. Some legislative proposals would employ thresholds of size and market share to establish the illegality of a particular acquisition or merger whether conglomerate, horizontal, or vertical. Thus, acquisitions or mergers involving firms above a certain size or with a certain percentage of the market could be successfully challenged without separate proof of the effect on prices and competition in the relevant market and without resort to subtle antitrust theory. Acquisitions and mergers involving firms and industries below the threshold limits would continue to be judged under existing antitrust theory and would be subject to the requirement of more specific proof of probable anticompetitive effect.

## Antitrust Theory Currently Advanced to Challenge Conglomerate Mergers

The Clayton Act and the Federal Trade Commission Act, which subsumes violations of the former act as unfair methods of competition, prohibit business acquisitions and mergers that may substantially lessen competition or tend to create a monopoly, and this prohibition applies to all mergers, horizontal, vertical, and conglomerate, alike. Congress has not spelled out appropriate standards by which to judge probable lessening of competition, nor has it established a clear and consistent rationale to serve as a touchstone in the interpretation of the statute in the context of actual cases. Thus, the courts have supplied operational content to the antimerger statutes in case-by-case adjudication with little guidance from Congress.

The principal thrust of the Sherman Act is punishment. The Clayton and Federal Trade Commission Acts are geared to prevent inappropriate acquisitions and mergers, and no specific intent to monopolize need be proved. The latter acts strike at incipient lessening of competition or creation of monopoly. Thus, acquisitions and mergers can be challenged more easily under these statutes than under the Sherman Act. This analysis will focus on challenges to mergers under the Clayton and Federal Trade Commission Acts, and the proposals discussed will include those that would amend these statutes.

Conglomerate mergers, unlike horizontal and vertical mergers, normally affect competition only indirectly. Consequently, "the economic and legal questions presented are generally more complex and elusive than those presented by horizontal and vertical acquisitions."[15] The theory of "potential competition" has been the most popular weapon against conglomerate mergers. Frequently a firm enters a field related to its existing activities, a field in which it has capability. Thus, some conglomerate mergers attacked under potential competition doctrine are "market extension" mergers (the firms involved produce the same product but they are not competitors since they operate in different geographical markets) or "product extension" mergers (the firms produce products that do not compete but which are functionally related in production or distribution). The two branches of potential competition doctrine are referred to as "perceived" potential competition and "actual" potential competition.

**Perceived Potential Competition Theory.** The perceived potential competition theory, as it has evolved through case-by-case adjudication, can only be applied if the relevant market of the firm acquired is substantially concentrated, and if the acquiring firm has the characteristics, capabilities, and economic incentive so that participants in the market will view it as a potential de novo entrant irrespective of its actual intent with respect to entry. As the Supreme Court has noted, the dominant participants in a concentrated market must be "engaging in interdependent or parallel behavior and with the capacity effectively to determine price and total output of goods or services," and the acquiring firm's position at the market edge must have "in fact tempered oligopolistic behavior on the part of existing participants in that market."[16]

In other words, the existing firms must have feared the introduction of greater supplies into the market, lower prices, and smaller market shares, should the perceived potential competitor enter and, because of this, they may behave competitively, that is, engage in limit pricing or other activities to discourage entry by the perceived potential entrant. Judicial reliance on the rationale that firms in an industry perceive that a firm on the edge of the market is a potential entrant is not based on the language of the statute but is derived from economic theory. The implication of this theory is that if the firm waiting on the edge of the market is allowed to acquire a firm in the market, the acquiring firm will not be perceived as a potential entrant thereafter, the other oligopolists will no longer have any reason to limit prices, and oligopolistic pricing will result, thus fulfilling theory as to the anticompetitive nature of the acquisition.[17]

**Actual Potential Competition Theory.** In the situation cited in the previous subsection, the perceived potential competitor confers benefits on the market *currently* as it stands on the edge of the market, thus forcing the major sellers in the market to charge less than an oligopolistic price. Under the actual potential competition theory, the competitive benefits lost by the potential entrant's acquisition of a major competitor already in the market are the *future* benefits that would be realized when the firm waiting in the wings to enter the market does so by de novo entry (expanding its own productive capacity to serve the market).[18]

Proponents of this theory claim these future benefits are twofold. If the firm waiting in the wings enters de novo, there will be an additional source of supply, more constraint on the market power of the firms already in the market, and a reduction in the possibility of collusion by the leading firms in the market. In the short run, de novo entry would inject an unsettling factor into the market. On the other hand, entry by acquisition of a leading firm already in the market leaves the same productive capacity as before and, assuming the lack of reciprocity and entrenchment (concepts discussed in succeeding subsections), market conditions will remain the same as before the acquisition.[19]

Antitrust plaintiffs clearly have difficult problems of proof to surmount in establishing the facts required to make out a case under the actual potential competition doctrine. The plaintiff, for example, must establish the defendant firm's intent to enter the market de novo within a reasonable time in the future when that firm actually entered by acquiring a major competitor in the market and now claims that it would not have considered any other option. In response to this particular problem of proof, the Federal Trade Commission developed the "toehold" doctrine—the acquisition by the firm waiting in the wings of a small toehold firm would have a procompetitive effect similar to that achieved by de novo entry. Although the toehold doctrine alleviates one of the plaintiff's problems of proof, it does not eliminate that problem entirely because adducing proof of intent to make toehold entry may still be difficult.[20]

Some critics charge that the actual potential competition theory is wrong, because acquisition of a leading firm already in the market causes no decline in competition. The acquiring firm is sued solely because it did not choose an alternative method of entry that would have yielded a more substantial increase in competition.[21] The Supreme Court has not yet endorsed the actual potential competition theory, although it has had opportunity to do so.[22]

**Entrenchment Theory.** The entrenchment theory is based on the premise stated by the Supreme Court in *FTC* v. *Procter & Gamble,* often referred to as the *Clorox* case, that the substitution of "a powerful acquiring firm for a smaller, but already dominant, firm may substantially reduce the competitive structure of the industry by raising entry barriers [to other firms wishing to enter] and by dissuading the smaller firms [in the industry] from aggressively competing."[23] Transfer of the economic power of the acquiring firm to the acquired firm is thus thought to "entrench" the market position of the acquired firm. This in turn may make the industry more oligopolistic and less competitive.[24] The Supreme Court's entrenchment ruling has been much criticized by antitrust scholars.[25]

**Probability of Reciprocal Dealing.** The Supreme Court case of *FTC* v. *Consolidated Foods Corp.* illustrates how the opportunity for reciprocal dealing provided by an acquisition is relied on to invalidate acquisitions and mergers in case-by-case adjudication.[26] The defendant, a substantial purchaser of products from food processors, acquired the manufacturer of 32 percent of the dehydrated onions and garlic. The acquired firm and another manufacturer together accounted for almost 90 percent of industry sales. The Court concluded that the defendant's threatened withdrawal of its orders for the products of other food processors, if they did not purchase dehydrated onions and garlic from its affiliate, and its conditioning of future purchases from these processors on the affiliate's receipt of orders from them for onions and garlic, constituted an anticompetitive practice. The possibility of minimal reciprocal buying would not justify remedial action against the merged firms. The Court concluded, however, that the merger carried the potential for extensive reciprocity as the defendant had the power to influence purchases of onions and garlic from its affiliate by a substantial segment of its own suppliers and, thus, the acquisition was unlawful even though the potential for reciprocity was not vigorously exploited. The Court cited the FTC's conclusion that reciprocal buying gave the defendant the power to foreclose competition from a substantial share of the market. Though the reciprocity theory has been criticized, it stands as a significant rationale for challenging conglomerate mergers affecting oligopolistic industries in circumstances comparable to those outlined in the *Consolidated Foods* case.[27]

**Other Theories.** Three additional theories have been proposed for use in attacking conglomerate mergers, though unsuccessfully. The first is a pure "deep pocket" theory, which is similar to the entrenchment theory, except that the acquired firm need not be dominant in the market.[28] It is based on the belief that a small firm in an industry supported by the economic power of a large outside firm will be able to eliminate competing small firms or reduce their share of the market. In this view, other firms, even if initially dominant in the market, will limit the vigor of their competition to avoid retaliation by the large acquiring firm. If this theory were generally accepted, it would substantially foreclose conglomerate acquisition by very large enterprises.

A second theory that has not been endorsed by the courts looks to the "competitive forbearance" that might flow from the proliferation of firms that face each other in numerous markets. Under this theory, a conglomerate would be more likely to rely on "soft competition" than a firm competing in a single industry for fear that aggressiveness in one market in which it holds a competitive edge over a conglomerate rival might be countered by reprisal in a second market in which the rival has the competitive advantage.[29]

A final theory, the most far-reaching approach suggested to overturn conglomerate mergers, is that of "aggregate concentration." This theory looks not to competitive effects in a particular market, but to the "concentration of assets and economic and political power in the hands of the major firms in the country. The concept involves not only the economic but also the social underpinnings of the antitrust laws."[30] Rarely raised, the theory has never been embraced by a judicial opinion and appears to have been rejected by two U.S. district courts.[31] Antitrust enforcement officials do not agree as to its validity.

## Court Construction of Clayton and Federal Trade Commission Acts

In a field in which so much of the practical effect of the antimerger laws depends on court interpretation, a brief discussion of the thrust of certain cases decided over the last two decades and the shifting requirements of proof of anticompetitive effect reflected in certain of these cases is necessary.[32] The first Supreme Court case decided following the 1950 amendment broadening the coverage of the Clayton Act to include conglomerate mergers was *Brown Shoe Company* v. *United States,* which involved both vertical and horizontal merger aspects.[33] In an opinion written by Chief Justice Earl Warren, the Court cited the concern of Congress in the 1950 amendments with a rising tide of mergers and the desire to stop them in their incipiency. It noted that during debate of the legislation some members of Congress spoke of the desirability of retaining local control over industry and of the protection of small businesses.[34] The Court chose, in terms of the standard of the proof required, an economic touchstone (legislative history shows a desire to restrain mergers "only to the extent" they "may tend to lessen competition"), but it did not spell out the standards by which an economic approach could be implemented. It referred to market share as a "primary index of market power," but it concluded that market share was just the beginning point for analysis, for it noted that the contents of the House committee report reflect "conscious avoidance of exclusively mathematical tests." Market power was not defined, nor did the Court state what weight was to be given to other factors.[35]

A year after its *Brown Shoe* decision, in an opinion written for five members of the Court by Justice William Brennan, *United States* v. *Philadelphia National Bank,* the Court took a much different view of the proof required to establish a merger's illegality.[36] The Court conceded that whether the effect of a merger may be substantially to lessen competition is not the kind of a question that is susceptible of a ready and precise answer in most cases. Prediction of the merger's impact on competitive conditions is only sound, the Court said, if it is based on knowledge of the structure of the market, but the relevant economic data are complex and elusive and, unless businesses can assess the legal consequences of a merger with some confidence, sound business planning is retarded. Thus, the Court dispensed with the requirement of "further examination" in the more clear-cut cases and resorted to a rebuttable presumption of illegality based on the merged firm's percentage of the market and the increased percentage controlled by the leading firms in the market. The merger there considered, which would produce a bank with 30 percent of the commercial banking in a four-county area and by which the two largest banks would control 33 percent more of the commercial banking business after the merger than was true before, presumptively lessened competition in violation of Section 7 of the Clayton Act. Thus, the Court sanctioned use of a mechanical test of concentration, a rule of presumptive illegality, that would simplify proof of illegality in many cases and ease problems of judicial administration.

In *United States* v. *Aluminum Co. of America,* decided the following year, the Court, in an opinion written by Justice William O. Douglas for six members, continued application of the mechanical test of market share and concentration adopted in the *Philadelphia National Bank* case.[37] Since the merger involved in the *Aluminum Company* case was horizontal, a small additional increase in concentration was sufficient, in the view of the Court, to find anticompetitive effect from the merger. In *United States* v. *Penn-Olin Chemical Company,* the Court used market share data and applied potential competition doctrine to reverse a court of appeals ruling that absolved a joint venture by leading companies in the sodium chlorate market of anticompetitive effect. The Court rejected the use of subjective evidence on the issue of whether or not elimination of either company's potential competition would substantially lessen competition, and it enumerated thirteen criteria to be examined by the trial court in determining the anticompetitive effect of the joint venture without stating the relative weight to be assigned to each factor.[38] Some critics of this decision felt that, unlike *Philadelphia National Bank,* this decision risked sinking the enforcement of judicial application of Section 7 of the Clayton Act into a morass of inscrutable, ambivalent, and even conflicting evidence that would adversely affect orderly judicial administration and make business planning an uncertain enterprise.[39] In the next case decided by the Court, *United States* v. *Continental Can Co.,* a majority of the Court largely ignored the economic evidence and concentrated on its view of the structural effect of the merger.[40]

The Court's opinion in *United States* v. *Von's Grocery Company,* written by Justice Hugo Black, involved the horizontal merger of two grocery chains in Los Angeles that produced a firm with 1.4 percent of the grocery stores in the area and 7.5 percent of sales.[41] The number of grocery chains had increased by 50 percent over a nine-year period, but the Court relied on the decline in the number of single-store owners to invalidate the merger. Some critics feared this decision signaled that any merger trend toward fewer competitors overall might be held illegal. *United States* v. *Pabst Brewing Company* marked an extension of the *Von's Grocery* rationale (a decline in the number of competitors and an increase in the share of the market controlled by the leading competitors) so that a horizontal merger producing a firm that controlled 4.49 percent of the national market (5.83 percent three years after the merger) was held invalid.[42]

The next major antimerger case to break significant new ground was *FTC* v. *Procter & Gamble,* in a decision written by Justice Douglas.[43] The product extension acquisition involved in that case was found to violate Section 7 of the Clayton Act because it enhanced the already dominant position of the acquired firm (Clorox) in the liquid bleach industry—entrenchment, or, as the Court put it, raising barriers to new entry—and because it eliminated Procter & Gamble as a potential competitor. The majority of the Court rejected the need for elaborate proof of probable anticompetitive effect, but it failed to establish standards regarding the size of the acquiring firm, the degree of dominance of the market by the acquired firm, or the status of the market necessary to show probable anticompetitive effect. In a separate opinion, Justice John Harlan complained that the majority opinion did not inform the FTC, lawyers, or businesses about what is expected of them in future cases of this kind.[44]

The Warren Court extended from 1954 to 1969, and through 1972 the government won all of its antimerger cases in the Supreme Court. By way of contrast, one antitrust enforcement official stated in late 1979 that there had not been a single unequivocal victory for either the government or private plaintiffs in Supreme Court cases challenging conglomerate mergers since 1973.[45]

The first significant shift in the direction of Supreme Court opinion after the Warren Court occurred in *United States* v. *General Dynamics Corporation* in an opinion written by Justice Potter Stewart, a frequent dissenter from Warren Court antimerger decisions.[46] The merger increased the market share of the two largest coal firms in two geographical markets, and there had been a sharp decline in the number of coal producers in one of the markets (compare the facts in the *Von's Grocery Company* case). Nevertheless, the Court concluded (as in *Brown Shoe Co.*) that market-share percentages are but the starting point of the "further examination" of the particular market (an examination requirement dropped in the *Philadelphia National Bank* case). Four justices dissented. Further examination convinced the Court that the acquired firm's market share overstated its competitive position since nearly all of its reserves were already committed under long-term contracts and no other reserves were available. The Court in *General Dynamics* spelled out the type of proof required for the rule of presumptive illegality that the Warren Court had devised in the *Philadelphia Bank* case. Until the *General Dynamics* case, some students of antitrust law thought that the failing-company doctrine was the only defense to the rule of presumptive illegality.

In *United States* v. *Marine Bancorporation,* the Supreme Court considered the government's arguments for applying potential competition theory to invalidate a bank merger.[47] The Court, in an opinion written by Justice Lewis Powell, concluded that state regulatory barriers were known to bankers. Thus, the out-of-town bank involved in the merger was not perceived as a competitor. In addition, the Court declined to rule on the actual potential competition theory presented by the government. It did outline at length the proof required to invalidate a merger under the perceived potential competition doctrine, including proof that the firm's premerger pressure on the target market in fact tempered oligopolistic behavior by those in the market. *Marine Bancorporation* now requires hard evidence based on economic data, and invocation of theory alone will not suffice to challenge mergers before the current Court.

More recently, in *Continental T.V. Inc.* v. *GTE Sylvania Inc.,* a Sherman Act case involving vertical market restrictions imposed by franchise agreements that prevent the sale of a manufacturer's television sets from outlets other than those specified in the agreements, the Supreme Court overruled the per se rule of illegality applied in an earlier decision of the Warren Court.[48] Justice Powell's decision for the majority noted that the earlier opinion contained no analytical support for the positions taken and that any departure from the rule-of-reason standard requiring full analysis must be based upon demonstrable *economic* effect.

The foregoing review of recent decisions of the Supreme Court illustrates the tension between sentiment for simplified rules for judging the illegality of conduct under the antitrust laws on the one hand and conviction on the other hand that detailed analysis of the economic consequences of mergers alone must be employed to judge illegality. The former approach is criticized by some scholars as invoking heroic simplicities to decide antitrust cases, declaring rules too sweeping and absolute to be followed in practice, and relying on factors of effect on social and political policy not within the rationale of current antitrust law. The latter is criticized for excluding consideration of political and social concerns that should be weighed by the courts, for increasing the cost of litigating antimerger cases, and for all but shutting down the successful challenge of conglomerate acquisitions and mergers. It is in this context that the debate over the proposals to restrict conglomerate mergers discussed in the next section is cast.

# 3

## Proposals to Restrict Conglomerate Mergers

The resurgence of merger activity during the 1970s, together with the mixed success of antitrust enforcement officials in limiting conglomerate mergers, have prompted several proposals for new antitrust legislation. The proposals are intended to halt most acquisitions by and between the largest corporations in the country.

### Antimerger Legislative Proposals

The most prominent recent legislative proposal is S. 600, the Small and Independent Business Protection Act of 1979, sponsored in the 96th Congress by Senator Edward M. Kennedy (D-Mass.), then chairman of the Senate Judiciary Committee, and a related bill, H.R. 3169, introduced by Representative John F. Seiberling (D-Ohio). As this is written, the highly publicized efforts of large firms seeking to acquire the Continental Oil Company (CONOCO) are expected to stimulate the reintroduction of these bills in the 97th Congress.[49] S. 600 would establish an absolute prohibition against mergers between corporations each of whose sales or assets exceed $2 billion. It would also ban any merger when the assets or sales of both merging firms exceed $350 million, or when one of the firms exceeds $350 million in sales or assets and the other has at least a 20 percent market share in a $100 million market, unless any of the following affirmative defenses applies:

- the merger would substantially enhance competition;
- the merger would result in substantial efficiencies (such as economies of scale in manufacturing, marketing, distribution, or research and development); or
- within one year before or after the transaction, the parties divest one or more going concerns with assets and revenues comparable to the assets and revenues of the smaller party to the merger.

Use of the affirmative defenses would be precluded if within the year before the merger either of the parties has been involved in another merger governed by the legislation. S. 600 would empower the attorney general and the FTC to enforce its provisions and would direct them to establish procedures enabling parties to a proposed merger to receive a binding determination of whether the merger satisfies any affirmative defense. The bill also authorizes private parties to seek injunctive relief. It does not allow for adjustment of its dollar thresholds to account for inflation, and it makes no mention of mergers involving foreign corporations.

The late Senator Philip Hart (D-Mich.) introduced his own bill, the Industrial Reorganization Act, that would make it unlawful for any corporation or two or more corporations to possess monopoly power in any line of commerce in any section of the country or with foreign nations. Monopoly power would be presumed, absent evidence to the contrary, under the following conditions:

- if the corporation's average rate of return on net worth after taxes is in excess of 15 percent over a period of five consecutive years out of the most recent seven years
- if there is no substantial price competition among two or more corporations in any line of commerce in any section of the country for a period of three consecutive years out of the most recent five-year period
- if any four or fewer corporations account for 50 percent or more of sales in any line of commerce in any section of the country in any year out of the most recent three-year period.

An Industrial Reorganization Commission would investigate possible violations and prosecute cases before an Industrial Reorganization Court.[50]

The White House Task Force on Antitrust Policy submitted a report (the Neal Report) July 5, 1968, recommending adoption of the Concentrated Industries Act.[51] Under this proposal, the attorney general would prosecute cases before a Special Antitrust Court against a firm or firms in a concentrated industry—that is, an industry in which four or fewer firms had an aggregate market share of 70 percent or more during at least seven of the previous ten years and four of the five most recent years. Firms with as little as 15 percent of the market share in a concentrated industry could be prosecuted. The court would take steps to reduce the market share of each defendant firm in the concentrated industry to not more than 12 percent in a reasonable time, not exceeding four years from the decree of relief.

A consultant employed by the FTC proposed a no-fault antimonopoly law to President Carter's National Commission to Review Antitrust Laws and Procedures. Although the executive order creating the commission restricted its work to the framework of existing antitrust law, the consultant advocated endorsement of a no-fault antimonopoly law as within the commission's mandate to find ways to expedite protracted antitrust litigation. The commission did not endorse a specific legislative proposal; it did, however, recommend congressional study of the no-fault monopoly concept.[52]

The Federal Trade Commission's Bureau of Competition advanced a proposal to restrict mergers during the Carter administration.[53] Its plan would prohibit any merger that produced a new corporation with an average of sales and assets greater than $2 billion. An otherwise prohibited merger would be permitted if the resulting corporation divested itself of a going concern of at least comparable value to the acquired firm. The divestiture would have to occur within one year of the merger (before or after). No spinoff would be required if the newly acquired firm's market value was less than $100 million. Under the FTC plan, all dollar threshold figures would be adjusted annually to account for inflation, and the purchase of a U.S. firm by a foreign firm would be exempt unless the average of the foreign firm's sales and assets in the United States exceeded $1 billion after the acquisition.

The Justice Department's Antitrust Division also advanced a plan during the Carter administration to restrict mergers.[54] Although no merger would be banned outright, the proposal would render presumptively unlawful any merger (1) when both parties exceed $100 million in sales or assets and the combined firm exceeds $2 billion in sales or assets, or (2) when one party exceeds $2 billion in sales or assets and the other has at least a 20 percent market share in a $100 million market with a four-firm concentration ratio exceeding 75 percent. The presumption of unlawfulness could be overcome upon a showing that the preponderant effect of the merger would be to enhance competition substantially.

## Other Proposals

In addition to the broad measures outlined above, less ambitious amendments to the antitrust laws have been proposed to help restrict mergers and acquisitions. Some scholars regard such plans as more attainable than sweeping antimerger measures. Other proposals would amend statutes other than the antitrust laws or would employ the rules process in an attempt to discourage merger activity.

Some antitrust advocates argue that the present antimerger statutes are broad enough to restrict conglomerate mergers if they are given the broad interpretation they deserve. An approach that would satisfy some of these advocates is legislation that would endorse existing theory advanced by antitrust plaintiffs to challenge conglomerate mergers and ease the burden of proving prohibited actions. One measure proposed is a bill to validate the actual potential competition doctrine that the Supreme Court has twice noted but has yet to endorse. Elizabeth Hanford Dole, for example, when she was a commissioner of the FTC, suggested that the Senate Judiciary Committee consider legislation endorsing the actual potential competition doctrine so that acquisitions and mergers involving firms with no immediate edge effect on the market but which are probable future entrants could be enjoined. It should be enough, in her view, to show that a firm would probably enter the market eventually—for example, when it could raise the necessary capital or when firms already in the market raised prices to a level that would make entry attractive. This, in her view, would make it easier to challenge a broader range of perhaps small, but significant, conglomerate mergers that threaten to eliminate the competition that such a future de novo or toehold-acquisition entrant could provide.[55]

An approach advocated by some scholars and antitrust plaintiffs calls for the FTC to issue a trade regulation rule under Section 5 of the Federal Trade Commission Act. FTC staff in fact proposed that the FTC publish advance notice of proposed rulemaking for a trade regulation rule that would supersede many of the judicially prescribed ground rules for the invalidation of product-extension and market-extension mergers that have been developed over the last twenty years. A violation of the FTC Act, under the suggested rule, would be presumed on the basis of such factors as the acquiring firm's size in sales and market ranking, the market share of the acquired firm, and the "proximity" of the relevant markets. The suggested rule would also outline the types of rebuttal evidence that would be considered as offsetting the presumption of violation. The FTC declined to issue the advance notice of proposed rulemaking, citing in its release of October 7, 1980, its reservations concerning this method of proceeding.[56]

Since U.S. tax laws and the recurrent depressed condition of the stock market encourage mergers, some argue that conglomerate mergers can be discouraged, or that deconcentration can be achieved, by changes in the tax laws and by the provision of incentives to encourage the voluntary split of conglomerates.[57]

Another school of thought holds that, if entry into an industry is relatively easy, oligopolists may set a price close to the competitive level. Greater attention, in this view, should be paid to reducing or eliminating barriers to entry so that entry will be facilitated or the threat of entry will force competitive pricing even in oligopolistic industries.[58]

Government regulatory agencies frequently limit entry into regulated industries or impose other barriers to effective competition. Most students of antitrust agree that reducing regulatory restrictions would aid in making the market more competitive which, after all, is the objective of antimerger proposals. Advocates of additional legislation to deal with conglomerate mergers acknowledge the merit of reducing regulatory barriers but deny that this is all that is required to ensure fully competitive conditions in concentrated industries.

# 4

## Issues and Arguments

### Economic Issues

**Conglomerate Mergers and Aggregate Concentration.** Proponents of measures to restrict conglomerate mergers believe that the conglomerate merger wave has contributed to rising aggregate concentration, defined as the share of all manufacturing or other economic activity controlled by the largest enterprises. Their statistical evidence is as follows: the 200 largest manufacturing corporations accounted for 48.2 percent of all U.S. manufacturing corporation assets in 1948, but 60 percent in 1972. Similarly, the *Fortune* 500 industrial corporations controlled 73 percent of the total assets of all manufacturing companies in 1972, but 83 percent in 1977. The percentage of all manufacturing assets held by manufacturing corporations with assets over $10 million, a group much larger than the *Fortune* 500, increased from 85 percent in 1968 to 87 percent in 1973 and to 89 percent in 1978. In the view of those supporting measures to restrict conglomerate mergers, these figures demonstrate that the largest industrial corporations hold a preponderant share of total manufacturing assets, and that the share is increasing at a consistent rate.[59]

Proponents admit that not all of the growth in asset share is traceable directly to mergers; their statistics show, however, that roughly half of the growth did result from mergers. The 200 largest manufacturing companies reported total assets of $399 billion in 1972. Their 1948 asset share, extrapolated to 1972, would have totaled only $320.5 billion. Therefore, the asset growth associated with the observed increase in asset share was $78.5 billion. During the 1948–1972 period, the 200 largest manufacturers acquired assets valued at the time of acquisition at $44.7 billion. Thus, slightly more than half—44.7/78.5—of asset share growth resulted from mergers.[60]

Advocates of measures to deal with conglomerate mergers contend that aggregate concentration is important because it increases the opportunity for anticompetitive behavior. They insist that concentration in a particular industry and concentration in other industries whose products may be used as substitutes for the products of the first industry are also important because concentration in a particular market is correlated with higher profits. Economist Joe Bain pioneered in the effort to prove the correlation of market concentration and profits in his 1951 study of 42 industries selected from the 340 industries for which census data was available.[61] In the three decades following, over fifty studies were made and a majority of these studies showed a generally positive relationship between market concentration and higher profit rates in the relevant industries.[62] Supracompetitive pricing, it is claimed, restricts output, diverts resources to second-best uses, and limits gross national product (GNP) to a lower figure than our national potential. Some estimates place lowered national output from this cause at approximately 6 percent of GNP.[63]

Opponents of measures to restrict conglomerate mergers disagree with the aggregate concentration figures cited above, with the proponents' analysis of the effect of merger activity upon aggregate concentration, with the statistical techniques used to calculate aggregate concentration, and with the very significance of aggregate concentration figures.

Opponents note that the asset share of the largest nonfinancial corporations actually declined between 1958 and 1975.[64] To support this, they rely on the statistics shown in table 1. Further, opponents argue, the share of after-tax corporate profits accounted for by the largest nonfinancial corporations has declined dramatically over the 1958–1975 period. In the case of the largest 200 firms, the share had declined from 73.9 percent to 39.2 percent. If in fact competition declines with increased concentration, then, according to opponents, expected monopoly practices have not been profitable in concentrated industries. A more plausible conclusion in their view is that competition is strong and, if anything, increasing.[65] Moreover, opponents claim that merger activity is unrelated to aggregate concentration. The 1967–1972 period, for example, was marked by the greatest merger wave of recent decades, yet aggregate concentration actually decreased. In contrast, the 1963–1967 period was characterized by limited merger activity, but aggregate concentration increased slightly.[66]

Author Peter Steiner's study of the growth in assets of the 200 largest firms between 1954 and 1968 shows that only 13 percent of this growth was from mergers. A 1969 FTC study found mergers to be responsible for 15.6 percent of the growth of the largest 200 firms during the 1950s. The Justice Department found that 22 percent of such growth resulted from mergers

TABLE 1

ASSETS OF THE 400 LARGEST NONFINANCIAL CORPORATIONS RELATIVE TO ALL NONFINANCIAL CORPORATE ASSETS

(percent)

| *Asset Group* | *1958* | *1963* | *1967* | *1972* | *1975* |
|---|---|---|---|---|---|
| Top 50 | 24.4 | 24.4 | 24.5 | 23.4 | 23.3 |
| Top 100 | 32.1 | 31.7 | 32.0 | 30.7 | 30.6 |
| Top 200 | 41.1 | 40.5 | 41.2 | 39.9 | 39.5 |
| Top 400 | 49.5 | 48.9 | 50.0 | 48.8 | 48.6 |

SOURCE: U.S. Congress, Senate, Subcommittee on Antitrust, Monopoly, and Business Rights of the Committee on the Judiciary, *Hearings on Mergers and Economic Concentration*, 96th Congress, 1st session, 1979, vol. 1, p. 146, statement of Alfred F. Dougherty, Jr.

during the 1972–1977 period. The U.S. Chamber of Commerce has calculated that a total ban on mergers from 1970 to 1976 would have diverted only 7.8 percent of asset growth from external to internal expansion.[67]

Opponents also believe that aggregate concentration figures are statistically inaccurate. Corporations are included in the aggregate concentration ratio for manufacturing if as much as 51 percent of their assets and sales relate to manufacturing. Because the largest corporations, more than the smaller ones, have tended to diversify into nonmanufacturing and foreign operations, measurement errors bias the claimed degree of industry concentration upward. When foreign and nonmanufacturing assets are stripped from the 46 percent share of manufacturing assets attributed to the 100 leading companies by the FTC in 1963, their share turns out to be 36 percent rather than 46 percent. In addition, six industries account for 30 percent of the value added in the U.S. economy, and thirty-five of the top fifty *Fortune* companies are in these industries. These six industries are characterized by capital-intensive manufactures whose efficiency depends on large scale, and reduction in size would sacrifice the economies of scale that benefit the economy and the consumers.[68]

More fundamentally, opponents argue that the aggregate concentration figures are conceptually meaningless, without any significance for important issues of public policy. First, there is no way to determine what the ideal level of aggregate concentration should be. Instead, the appropriate level must depend on the economic aims of the nation. It has been suggested, for example, that, if we wish to increase our export trade, aggregate concentration should be higher than it currently is; but if we wish to increase our production of food, clothing, and textiles, aggregate concentration should be lower than it is.[69] Second, aggregate concentration figures do not accurately measure "economic power." The economy is composed of separate markets, and economic power that does not manifest itself in monopoly power in a particular market cannot manifest itself elsewhere in the economy. "No economist would regard a 20-firm concentration ratio of, say, 50 percent as necessarily indicative of power in a particular market. By analogy, a 50, 100, or 200 firm concentration ratio in the economy as a whole would not be indicative of power in the economy as a whole."[70]

Economist Joseph Schumpeter of Harvard University concluded that the fundamental impulse that keeps the capitalistic engine in motion comes from new consumer goods, new methods of production or transportation, new markets, and new forms of industrial organization. He defended large-scale enterprises as advancing progress most conspicuously and noted that inquiry concerning the source of individual items that contributed most to progress leads to the doors of big business.[71] Schumpeter's pupil, economist John Kenneth Galbraith, argues that firms of large size are essential for effective planning and development, and that it is appropriate that the largest corporations should approximate the size of governments. Galbraith contends, moreover, that most of the cheap and simple inventions have been made and development is now so sophisticated and costly that firms must be large enough to average out successes and failures because few firms can afford development if they must expect all projects to pay off. A modern industry of a few larger firms, in his view, is an almost perfect instrument for inducing technical change. Such industry is admirably equipped for financing technical development, and it has strong incentives for undertaking development and pursuing it to completion.[72] Students of merger motives note that horizontal mergers create additional market power, which adds to concentration in particular industries (whereas conglomerate mergers do not), and, if market power were the dominant motive for mergers, most mergers would be horizontal or would involve firms in concentrated industries, but neither of these circumstances obtain.[73]

Opponents note that even Bain in his pioneering work on the relation of industry concentration in particular markets to industry profits acknowledged that some firms may be more efficient and thus gain a larger share of the market even under conditions of perfect competition and that some degree of concentration will result from economies of large-scale firms.[74] Economist Yale Brozen of the University of Chicago examined the analysis Bain employed to show a correlation between industry concentration and higher profits and supplemented that analysis to determine if higher profits persisted over time (the thesis of President Johnson's Task Force on Antitrust Policy). Brozen expanded the sampling of industries studied and found that the correlation of higher profits and concentration did not persist. The correlations degenerated within a few years, and high and low profit rates tended to converge toward a common level. This and other studies challenging Bain's findings are cited by opponents of conglomerate legislation to show that correlations between concentration and profit rates can be attributed to variations in the size of the firms and not to the degree to which markets are concentrated; large-scale firms enjoy economies of scale or otherwise prove to be more efficient.[75]

In recent decades, transportation and communication have improved steadily and remarkably so that firms that once sold only regionally now sell nationwide or even worldwide thus bringing more firms into direct competition; buyers are more willing to travel distances to purchase their goods and, as buyers are better informed through radio, television, and the telephone, this facilitates competition. Opponents of measures to restrict conglomerate mergers contend, moreover, that such mergers strengthen competition. The acquisition of a firm in an industry new to a conglomerate, it is claimed, is likely to add competitive vigor to the market; reinvigoration of the acquired company improves performance and improves service to buyers. A battle of giants is better for competition than a skirmish of pygmies. Large firms keep close track of their rank in sales and fight hard to move ahead of rivals (or to avoid being surpassed by rivals), and competition among large firms is stimulated by their greater capacity for technological research.[76]

Opponents contend that measures to restrict conglomerate mergers would penalize firms that competed according to the rules and were successful. Bills such as S. 600 force companies at the levels of size set forth in the bill to avoid internal growth that might bring them within the ambit of the legislation. Such a system of arbitrary restraints would substitute government planning for the action of the market in determining, through the rewards and punishments of business risk, the evolutionary path of U.S. business. Government would set firm size without regard to the need for greater size in some industries than in others and without adjustment for future inflation. The idea that government should prohibit the creation of firms of certain sizes without proof of harm to the public in the specific cases, just because the bill sponsors prefer a different kind of social and economic structure, is, according to opponents of no-fault conglomerate legislation, a radical idea.[77]

Advocates of measures to restrict conglomerate mergers respond to claims that aggregate concentration has not increased substantially in recent years by noting that the growth of the economy works to deconcentrate industries within the economy but that conglomerate mergers have prevented normal deconcentration by this means. Advocates dispute the claim that large-size firms are needed to perform the planning function as claimed by Galbraith and to advance innovation and development as asserted by Schumpeter. Rather, they claim, the unit of technical efficiency is the plant and not the firm, and conglomerates frequently have a series of plants. A firm producing divergent lines of products may be seeking conglomerate size and power but in doing this it certainly is not responding to technological necessity. Firms can probably be counted on to move to optimal-scale plants rather quickly even without mergers.[78] Proponents' arguments against the necessity of large size to promote innovation are detailed in the subsection below on Innovation.

According to advocates, the claim that firms in concentrated industries cannot charge supracompetitive prices because this will attract new competitors into the market ignores the problems potential competitors have in overcoming barriers to entry. Where there are significant barriers to entry into a market served by a concentrated industry, it is argued, the firms in the industry can charge higher prices without fear of significant new competition. Advocates respond to the argument that other products will compete for the consumers' purchases if firms in a concentrated industry keep prices high, by citing Donald Turner's conclusion that, even though aluminum wire competes with copper wire, this does not mean that concentration in one of these industries has no impact on the price of its commodities or on other aspects of competitive performance.[79] Advocates contend that the studies challenging Bain's theory concerning the correlation between concentration and higher prices have not done much damage to that thesis, for many studies covering the same years have shown a strong relationship between concentration and prices in individual industries.[80] Some advocates maintain that if such legislation is not enacted the time may come when the government will be required to impose price or profit regulation on concentrated industries, but that it is much better to make competition work with the aid of their legislative proposal.[81]

Opponents of measures to restrict conglomerate mergers note that economists who have accepted the thesis that there is a correlation between concentration in an industry and higher prices concede that, if entry barriers are not high, even firms in a cartel will eventually earn only competitive rates of return on investment. Some industries lack significant barriers to entry, opponents claim; in the case of the meat-packing industry, for example, it is sometimes said that "a rope and a knife are all you need to go into this business" and that large established firms have been overtaken by smaller aggressive firms with plants closer to the source of supply.[82] Insofar as entry barriers are claimed to permit higher prices in concentrated industries, opponents of conglomerate legislation contend that, if entry barriers are examined analytically, it is seen that they have often been defined too expansively and that only the "differentially higher cost borne by a new entrant" should be considered as an entry barrier. So considered, entry barriers do not present a major problem to new entry, and firms already in a concentrated industry charging supracompetitive prices will either have to cut prices or surrender market share to new entrants or to smaller firms already in the market that can expand output without significantly higher capital costs than the larger firms.[83]

The truly troublesome entry restrictions, according to opponents of conglomerate legislation, are the myriad of entry restrictions embodied in federal, state, and local laws and regulations. Too often, government commissions that start out to regulate wind up protecting the established firms in the market; the power to license becomes the power to exclude; and the supervision of business practices becomes a pretext for harassing the weaker firms that can least afford these extra burdens and costs in their quest for greater market share, a quest that would add to competition and reduce concentration in the marketplace.[84] Thus, opponents insist that advocates' time would be better spent in eliminating governmentally imposed restraints on entry and competition.

**Conglomerates and the Potential for Anticompetitive Conduct.** Proponents of measures to restrict mergers believe that large conglomerate mergers pose significant anticompetitive threats, even if no single transaction would violate traditional antitrust standards. In particular, it is feared that large conglomerates might (a) practice cross-subsidization or create a deep pocket, enabling the firms to eliminate smaller rivals; (b) raise barriers to entry and eliminate potential competition; (c) engage in reciprocal dealing and mutual forbearance; and (d) frighten smaller firms into less vigorous rivalry.

Opponents, in contrast, believe that such fears are based on flawed economic logic. Either conglomerates lack the power to engage in anticompetitive conduct or the conduct would be irrational from their standpoint. In any event, opponents contend that the preventive legislation such as S. 600 is far too drastic a measure for the relatively rare instances of anticompetitive behavior that would be prevented, and that the proposed legislation would do nothing to prevent these practices by firms below a certain size that may be particularly strong in certain regional or local markets.

*Cross-subsidization and deep pocket.* Cross-subsidization occurs when a multimarket firm or geographically dispersed conglomerate employs profits earned in one market to finance competitive losses in another market—losses presumably sustained in anticipation of supranormal profits after competitors in a particular market are eliminated. Corwin Edwards, former chief economist at the FTC, popularized the view that conglomerates have "deep pockets," from which they can finance predatory practices. In this view, large firms—with large war chests—can hold prices below costs in some markets until smaller, less affluent rivals have been eliminated. Economist Walter Adams contends that conglomerate power derives not from monopoly or oligopoly control of a particular market, but from diversification over a whole range of markets that enables the firm with a deep purse to, in the words of Edwards, "outbid, outspend, and outlose" its smaller rivals.[85] Proponents of measures to restrict conglomerate mergers contend that the conglomerate "occupies a position much like the millionaire poker player who, in a game of unlimited stakes, can easily bankrupt his less opulent opponents."[86]

The threat of cross-subsidization is perceived to be greatest in an industry composed primarily of single-line firms that lack other markets from which they, too, could cross-subsidize.[87] After acquiring a firm with a small market share in such an industry, a conglomerate would have strong incentive to practice cross-subsidization to increase its share. Price and nonprice rivalry would escalate, forcing prices below cost and devastating the smaller, less affluent firms in the industry. Borrowing from former Congressman Emanuel Celler (D-N.Y.), proponents suggest that in this structural setting "the conglomerate that argued it was merely engaging in hard competition was like the elephant that said, 'every man for himself,' as he danced among the chickens."[88] Small firms and even rivals of nearly equal size, it is argued, would have to adopt pricing below cost or risk losing sales volume to the initiator of predatory pricing and thus fall far behind that rival in the competitive race.[89]

Antitrust scholars acknowledge the difficulty of devising a rule that will distinguish between undesirable predatory price reductions on the one hand and desirable procompetitive price reductions on the other. The pending legislation does not address this difficulty but rather seeks to prevent mergers and thus, in its proponents' view, reduces opportunity for predatory pricing.

Some opponents admit that large, multimarket firms may be capable of injuring small rivals through predatory pricing or deep-pocket financing. Opponents maintain, however, that instances of attempted predation are rare and successful predation is quite unlikely.[90] Competing firms may differ in assets and financial resources in terms of their absolute size but, according to opponents, their available resources are often proportional to their size, and this is sufficient to defeat an attempt at predation. Credit is generally available to firms seeking to withstand an attempt at predation and the deep-pocket effect simply cannot occur if there are rival firms large enough to withstand intimidation. Turner claims, for example, that the predator should have fifteen times the amount of assets of the next largest firm in the market for deep pocket to apply.[91]

Opponents argue that predatory pricing rarely makes economic sense: the practice is profitable only if losses sustained during the period of price cutting required to secure essentially a monopoly position in the market are more than outweighed by supracompetitive profits earned after effective competition has been eliminated. At one time, predation was attempted to convince a rival firm to merge, but the restrictions on horizontal mergers are now so stringent, opponents maintain, that this motive for predation has all but been eliminated. (The *Pabst Brewing* case, for example, bars a combined firm with nearly 4.5 percent of the market.) Opponents cite several reasons why losses during the period of price cutting will rarely be recouped through subsequent supracompetitive prices. First, the predator must win the price war quickly to have a reasonable expectation that future gains will outweigh present losses, but even with superior resources the predator's financial condition is likely to worsen more rapidly than that of its smaller competitors. This is so, according to Robert H. Bork, former solicitor general of the United States, because the predator must increase output to satisfy the new demand stimulated by its lower prices and to take up the market relinquished by its competitors. Increased production will mean that the predator will have higher average variable costs while the competitors' variable costs are moving lower.[92] Second, opponents contend that conglomerates normally cannot subsidize predatory pricing practices from sales in other markets and regions because the predator is already maximizing profits in all markets and it will have no way of increasing profits elsewhere to finance predation. Third, the difficulty of offsetting present losses with future earnings is compounded by the fact that the costs of present losses are immediate but anticipated monopoly profits will only be realized in the future and must be discounted by the rate of interest because they are not now available to cover the losses.[93]

The improbability that future earnings will be enough to offset price-cutting losses for the predator is further demonstrated, opponents maintain, by the fact that substitute products will normally be found that compete in the market so that the predator cannot charge supracompetitive prices. Supracompetitive prices will attract new entrants into the market. New entrants will bid down the price to a competitive level, and the attempt to recoup sums lost by price cutting will fail. The predator can exclude rivals following the price war only if it continues to price below cost or if it can erect barriers to entry, something that is feasible in only a few markets. If the predator is successful in defeating a rival in the market, the rival can reorganize in bankruptcy and emerge with debts scaled down so that it can compete anew or it may be purchased by a conglomerate with resources to defeat the attempt at predation.

In sum, predatory price cutting makes little sense, according to opponents of conglomerate legislation, and the law need not be amended to discourage predatory tactics. The efficiency loss from the proposed change would far exceed the benefits that could be gained under the most optimistic estimates of the benefits of making predatory price cutting more impossible.[94]

*Entry barriers and potential competition.* Proponents of measures to restrict conglomerate mergers claim that such mergers raise entry barriers, because firms are reluctant to enter industries in which they will face a conglomerate rival. Similarly, proponents claim that the mergers have reduced potential competition in certain industries. They point, for example, to a loss of potential competition in the steel industry when LTV acquired Jones and Laughlin, the sixth largest steel company, rather than entering through internal expansion or the acquisition of a small steel firm.[95]

Proponents admit that, in principle, current antitrust doctrine prohibits mergers where such anticompetitive effects are likely to ensue. The problems are evidentiary: present law sets such difficult standards of proof that it does not effectively bar mergers with proscribed effects.

Opponents argue that conglomerate mergers do not raise entry barriers, except where the mergers produce efficiencies. Where efficiencies do result, it is argued, public policy should favor the merger.[96] Where efficiencies have not resulted, there is little reason to believe that other firms—and especially other large firms—will be cowed by the presence of conglomerates. Firms will seek to enter highly profitable markets, just as they always have done. To the extent that entry barriers may be raised, opponents believe that entrenchment remains a valid ground for antitrust intervention. Indeed, in their view the standard of proof is so low as to block mergers without perceptibly harmful effects.

Similarly, opponents believe that current antitrust doctrine and standards of proof are adequate to prohibit conglomerate mergers that would result in a loss of potential competition. They admit that the theory contains a kernel of truth.

*Mutual forbearance.* Proponents of conglomerate legislation urge its adoption to limit the opportunities for mutual forbearance. Mutual forbearance from ardent competition occurs, it is claimed, when conglomerate firms are aware that they meet in numerous markets and in varying competitive and cooperative relationships and find it mutually advantageous to accept implicit spheres of influence or to avoid hard competition. Such firms will be less prone to press their advantage in markets where they have a competitive edge for fear of retaliation in markets where they are at a competitive disadvantage. "The current merger movement has greatly increased the 'contact points' among large corporations and, therefore, the likelihood that conglomerates will exercise forbearance in their competitive confrontations."[97] The ultimate result of increased conglomeration, proponents fear, would be a system resembling the Zaibatsu system in Japan, in which a limited number of huge conglomerates are immune from the disciplining influence of the market and instead work in concert with the state to exercise great control over many key economic and political decisions. Such a system, it is claimed, would be quite inconsistent with the American tradition of free enterprise and the discipline of the marketplace.

Opponents of measures to restrict conglomerate mergers do not regard mutual forbearance, accepting its existence for sake of argument, as a serious economic threat. They doubt that corporate interdependence is increased by conglomerate mergers. The economy is composed of numerous markets, and economic power, including oligopolistic interdependence, in their view, manifests itself in these individual markets. A conglomerate merger substitutes one corporate entity for another, but it does not increase concentration in the individual markets or interdependence in any particular market. Rather, conglomerate acquisitions and mergers are likely to step up rivalry. Certainly, a conglomerate acquisition cannot increase interdependence at the same time it increases rivalry. Opponents note that even Phillip Areeda and Donald Turner, who have written of the *possibility* of mutual forbearance, admit that conglomerate mergers seldom produce the kind of interdependence that may lead to mutual forbearance and that the circumstances in which mutual forbearance may occur are limited. Areeda and Turner note, moreover, that even oligopoly (which is more likely to produce an anticompetitive atmosphere than is conglomerate merger) seldom, if ever, diminishes technological or innovational competition. They conclude: "We can state with reasonable confidence . . . because the incidence and importance of extended interdependence are so doubtful, the mere assertion that mutual forbearance is a possible consequence of conglomerate mergers does not provide sufficient justification for condemning these mergers."[98]

*Reciprocity*. Proponents of measures to restrict conglomerate mergers contend that reciprocal buying is common among conglomerates since the large and varied assortment of goods and services purchased by a conglomerate can be used as leverage in making sales. Reciprocity—defined as "taking your business to those who bring their business to you"—it is claimed, stultifies competition to the detriment of excluded sellers. Corwin Edwards contends that, "since leverage in reciprocity increases with the enterprise's aggregate purchases, small firms may become satellites of their largest customers, and large firms reciprocally derive strength as sellers from their bigness as buyers. Bigness fosters still more bigness."[99] Proponents argue that reciprocal buying will occur whenever firms have both incentive and opportunity for reciprocity. The incentive exists when increased profits are possible—most likely in a market of relatively few sellers. Opportunity merely requires that one firm produce something used by the other. Willard Mueller, former chief economist at the FTC, refers to reciprocity as "the inevitable concomitant of an economy in which most commerce is controlled by a relatively few huge corporations."[100]

Opponents of measures to restrict conglomerate mergers maintain that reciprocity is not a genuine economic threat. Current antitrust law is adequate in their view to enjoin conglomerate mergers that are likely to result in reciprocal dealing.[101] Opponents argue that reciprocal dealing would occur even if there were no conglomerates. Enactment of the pending legislation would not eliminate the practice. They contend that a merger has no effect on reciprocal buying, since a firm can use its buying power to obtain favorable terms for the goods it sells only once. The firm, if it was using such buying power as it had before merger, would have no leverage left to "coerce any unwarranted favors for [an affiliate] after the merger. The theory [of reciprocity] is another instance of the fallacy of counting the same market power twice."[102]

*Intimidation of smaller rivals*. Proponents of measures to restrict conglomerate mergers contend that the creation of large conglomerates chills the willingness of small firms to compete significantly in price. In this view, a small firm that had formerly competed vigorously would consider itself outgunned: it could not win a competitive battle against a mammoth conglomerate, so it would be wise not to initiate a skirmish. Edwards maintains: "A big conglomerate that becomes a price leader seldom needs to use threats, and even more seldom needs to take overt disciplinary action. Most small rivals can be coerced by their own imaginations."[103]

Opponents, in contrast, doubt that conglomerates are capable of frightening small firms into less vigorous rivalry; if anything, the opposite effect occurs. The small firm's existence hinges on its success in a single market, and it is likely to fight fiercely to preserve its share, particularly if threatened by an outside intruder. Small firms also are more likely to be managed by persons with sentimental attachment to a particular industry, persons who will be less likely than professional managers to submit to market discipline and will fight vigorously to preserve their standing within the industry. Small firms may also have the advantage of specialization, the production of items with short production runs to take advantage of product differentiation, and their service to small geographical markets may give them competitive advantages, particularly as transportation expenses become a greater cost factor for conglomerates. Furthermore, if the industry is sufficiently oligopolistic to be subject to market discipline enforced merely by the looming presence of a conglomerate parent of one member firm, one must wonder why the industry did not tap its oligopolistic potential—and limit its rivalry—earlier.[104]

**Conglomerates: Innovation and Capital Formation.** Proponents of measures to restrict conglomerate mergers argue that such mergers reduce both innovation and capital formation. In contrast, opponents believe that measures to restrict conglomerate mergers will reduce innovation and discourage capital formation.

*Innovation.* Economists such as Schumpeter and Galbraith have argued that large firm size is necessary for optimal advancement of technology through innovation and development. On the other hand, proponents of measures to restrict conglomerate mergers cite evidence suggesting that the greatest level of research intensity emerges from solo inventors and from small- and medium-sized firms, rather than from giant corporations. One study, for example, suggests that economies of scale for innovation could be found in firms up to 5,000 employees, but not beyond that. Another observed that of sixty-one basic inventions examined, only sixteen resulted from research by large corporations.

> For example, the ballpoint pen was invented by a sculptor, the dial telephone by an undertaker. The firms which introduced stainless steel razor blades (Wilkinson), transistor radios (Sony), photocopying machines (Xerox), and the "instant" photograph (Polaroid) were all small and little known when they made their momentous breakthroughs.[105]

The best explanation for these empirical phenomena, according to proponents, is that firms which already dominate an industry have little incentive to risk funds on speculative research ventures.

F.M. Scherer acknowledges that in a few instances large size may be necessary. Very few companies in the world, for example, have the know-how, resources, reputation, and market access to develop a Boeing 747. But Scherer contends that even firms that are too small to support a laboratory may have no trouble employing the most up-to-date technology and, in such cases, the size of the firm may have little or no bearing on either the rate of technological progress or the balance of strategic advantage between large and small users. Scherer contends, moreover, that the sluggishness of large firms in recognizing and rewarding innovative ideas may drive innovative personnel to smaller firms where their proposals have a better chance of receiving personal consideration by the top decision maker.[106] Walter Adams contends that there is no strict correlation between large size and progressiveness. In fact, he states, it was a small steel firm rather than the large firms that first employed the basic oxygen furnace for steelmaking in this country.[107]

Advocates claim that conglomerate mergers are doubly threatening: not only do large firms result, but as "alternative or competing technologies are increasingly brought under common control, there may be significant incentives to suppress one technological approach and concentrate on another, while both would likely have been developed if the firms had remained independent."[108] With a large number of independent decision-making units, there is less chance that an important technological advance will be blocked by the faulty judgment of a few men.[109]

Opponents of measures to restrict conglomerate mergers cite the views of scholars such as Schumpeter, Galbraith, and Henry Villard that the costs of innovation and development are so large that firms of large size are best equipped to carry on such activities and that successes and failures average out for a large firm, whereas a small firm is not in a position to weather failures. Just as the prospect of a commanding position in an industry raises the odds in favor of the most risky innovations, so bigness makes possible the most expensive innovations. Just as large firms can hedge against technical uncertainties associated with innovation by undertaking several projects at once, the diversified conglomerate is more likely to find use, and a broader range of uses, for the uncertain outcome of research and development projects than will a single-product firm that may not be able to exploit an invention that is not directly linked to its primary product. Harold Geneen, president of International Telephone and Telegraph (ITT), contends that a conglomerate has numerous specialists and experienced managers in many fields and that the very untraditional outlook such a firm brings to an industry is the key to innovation and new progress. The quest for a commanding position in an industry, it is claimed, leads to innovation, while the fear of loss of position by the large firm promotes continued innovation and the adoption of new technology. A large firm may be shaken by the introduction of new products by its competitors, but because it is large it is better able, and more likely, to fight back with its own research, capital resources, and know-how and to secure a place in industry competition.[110]

Opponents of conglomerate legislation acknowledge that empirical data on the relationship between firm size and innovation is mixed. This is true, it is claimed, because the need for innovation varies from industry to industry, depending on the kind of markets served by the industries. A conglomerate is not likely to pour major R & D dollars into a mature product line with a go-nowhere future.[111] Opponents argue, however, that the reward of large profits in the mature stage of a product line (or the penalty of losing out on those profits) induces firms to build volume of sales as early as possible and to "race down the experience curve to secure a favorable cost position." The large profits that may be earned by the firm with a strong position in the mature stage of a product line, it is claimed, spur a higher level of investment in innovation, especially since the innovating firm may gain a head start in the race down the experience curve.[112] Over 80 percent of all private research and development is undertaken by the largest manufacturing corporations. Large firms also spend more on research and development as a fraction of sales. "This suggests that an upper absolute limit in firm growth by merger involves some risk of slowing down our rate of technological progress."[113]

In most industries, it is claimed, there is a threshold for the size of an efficient program of research and development. If firms are not large enough to support a program of minimum effective size, their efforts are ad hoc and informal or largely nonexistent. Some contend that, when a smaller firm runs into difficulty, its R & D budget is the first expenditure to be eliminated. Even when firms do not compete vigorously with prices, they will continue to compete with technical innovation, one of the most important weapons of market rivalry. No expenditures, it is claimed, are more competitive than outlays on research. Only large firms have the resources to engage in basic research on a significant scale. Thus, Jesse Markham claims that Schumpeter's thesis, at a high level of generalization, has met the test of factual analysis.[114]

Even assuming that small- and medium-size firms are the most innovative, opponents argue, the legislation would discourage formation of, or innovation by, small firms and would penalize risk-taking. Venture capitalists evaluating a proposed investment seriously consider the means of recouping that investment. "One major incentive that fuels the entrepreneurial spirit and the growth of small firms," according to Donald I. Baker, former assistant attorney general for the Antitrust Division, "is their ability to sell out at a profit once they become successful."[115] Opponents note that even proponents admit that a "market for acquisitions increases incentives for investment in closely held corporations, because purchase of all stock by a merger partner may provide the only financially viable method for sale of the company where there are difficulties involved in disposing of large blocks of stock held by a firm's owners on the open market."[116] Any restriction on the ability to recoup one's investment in the acquisition market will limit the incentive to undertake an investment in the first place.

A merger may be the only means by which a small firm can acquire additional funds with which to complete its innovative activity. Often a small firm will have exhausted its capital before it has completed the development and marketing of its product or service. In addition, opponents argue that arbitrary size ceilings would create disincentives for small firms' attempting to grow as rapidly as they otherwise would, and this would itself discourage innovation.[117]

*Capital formation.* Proponents of the legislation argue that conglomerate mergers result in lower rates of capital formation: instead of constructing new plants, large firms, by acquiring other firms through conglomerate acquisitions, are making "sterile investments that create nothing new." Consequently, productive capacity stagnates and the nation's economic growth slows.[118] Economist Dennis C. Mueller of the University of Maryland, in testifying concerning a bill that would limit acquisitions by oil companies, stated:

> Since growth and diversification are the primary objectives behind [conglomerate] mergers, blocking this form of external expansion should lead to greater investments to bring about growth and diversification through internal expansion.[119]

Proponents hope that restricting mergers as proposed in the pending legislation will shift corporate investment from conglomerate acquisitions to investment in new productive capacity.

Opponents, on the other hand, believe that conglomerate mergers have little effect on the rate of capital formation in the economy. To the extent that any effect might be theorized, mergers would increase capital formation. Under national income accounting procedures, the amount of capital available for investment in the economy over any period of time equals the national savings during that time. The principal effect of a merger is to alter the location of the savings: one firm uses its savings to acquire another firm and transfers those savings to the individuals who previously owned the acquired firm. Although the location has changed, the total amount of savings in the economy has remained unchanged. Hence, the potential for new investment has remained unchanged as well.[120]

Opponents believe that the legislation can only dampen the rate of capital formation. Because the legislation would dampen the acquisitions market, sources of venture capital would face lower expected return and greater risk. This would reduce the incentive to save, and the level of investment would be reduced accordingly.[121]

Opponents maintain, moreover, that a merger with a larger company may be the only cost-effective means by which a small firm can raise funds for expansion or survival. Public stock issues are very costly to small entrepreneurs and, as long as the equity markets are rotten, the merger market offers the small entrepreneur the only realistic way to raise funds to modernize and grow. Conglomerate acquisition of a small firm under such circumstances, even according to advocate John H. Shenefield, may have procompetitive benefits.[122] Indeed, opponents claim that conglomeration, in addition to reducing capital-raising costs in the market, may make better use of internally generated funds because the conglomerate can transfer funds from units operating at a surplus to units operating at a deficit. Bork thus contends that conglomerate mergers provide one of the means by which the capital market overcomes its alleged "imperfections." Turner contends that conglomeration increases the rewards of a successful entrepreneur, who can sell out to or merge with a larger firm, and this stimulates the formation and growth of new firms, which is procompetitive.[123]

**Conglomerate Mergers and Efficiency Gains.** Opponents argue that the legislation will prevent capital from reaching its most productive uses. In their view, a free market economy results in the efficient allocation of capital. J. Fred Weston contends that mergers reprice assets in the marketplace, thereby facilitating improved use of economic resources. When the market for capital assets functions efficiently, the economy operates more flexibly and efficiently. According to Weston, there is no more reason to restrict the operation of the market for capital assets, as proposed in the pending legislation, than there is to devise new restrictions on the labor market, on the financial markets, or on markets for individual products.[124] Although a particular conglomerate merger may be undertaken to increase profitability, the profitability change merely reflects efficiency gains. Were Congress to restrict conglomerate mergers, the argument continues, particular applications of capital would be barred. Among those applications are certain to be many that would increase efficiency.

The forms of efficiency gain that opponents attribute to conglomerate mergers fall into three basic classes: improvement of management competence; reduction in the cost of management, capital, production, product development, and marketing and promotion; and paper efficiencies such as tax benefits and accounting gimmicks.

Because the legislation shelters corporate management from the threat of takeover, opponents contend, waste and inefficiency may result. Mergers are seen as a typical device by which incompetently or suboptimally managed corporate assets are reallocated to more efficient managers. The current treatment of conglomerate mergers produces efficiency gains in two ways. First, if assets are poorly managed, they will be taken over by more competent managers. The same assets will be made more productive, resulting in efficiency gains. Second, the mere threat of takeover stimulates corporate managers to remain vigorous and cost-conscious. Should proposed legislation remove the threat and therefore the stimulus, managers would be lulled into complacency. Our financial markets, according to opponents, will reward efficient management and punish inefficient management, if it is allowed to function freely without the proposed constraints on mergers and acquisitions.[125] The possibility of a takeover keeps the management of target firms alert. Prohibiting mergers and takeovers as proposed, according to Weston, would make entry into new industries difficult and would adversely affect competition, prices of products, quality of products, and innovation.[126]

Conglomerate mergers may also produce operating efficiencies, sometimes referred to as "synergies"—that is, the cooperative action of the units in a conglomerate will produce greater total results than the sum of the results of the various units acting independently. A conglomerate merger is less likely to result in production efficiencies than is a horizontal or vertical merger. Such efficiencies may, however, be achieved in some cases where common production facilities can be employed to achieve economies of large scale.[127] Improved efficiencies and cost reductions can also be achieved by conglomerates in the areas of management, marketing and promotion, engineering and product development, staffing, legal and other activities, and finance. Management efficiencies may be achieved through more dynamic leadership, through integrated forward planning, by spreading improved management capabilities and expertise over a wider range of activities, by better monitoring, and, in some cases, by eliminating duplicate management positions. The acquiring firm may have an established distribution network through which the products of the acquired firm can also be marketed. Marketing and promotional efficiencies may be achieved because of quantity discounts for advertising, the utilization of superior promotional experience of the acquiring company, or because of a strong trademark, for example.[128] Centralized procurement may produce economies, and product development economies may be achieved through the consolidation of complementary R & D activities, the elimination of duplicate facilities, or the facilitated transfer of proprietary information across traditional industry lines among the firms in the conglomerate family.[129] Weston contends that diversification through conglomerate acquisitions provides a base of greater stability and reduced uncertainty, thus lessening the possibility of bankruptcy losses and making greater innovation and new product development possible. Diversification is important, in his view, because of the pace of technological change, shortened life cycles for products, and the greater difficulty of forecasting the impact of changes in particular industries.[130]

Perhaps the efficiency most frequently realized by conglomerate firms is in acquiring and using capital. The efficiency may arise in three ways. First and most critically, a conglomerate merger reduces risk through diversification. Risks are "pooled" by pairing firms that do not respond with perfect correlation to fluctuations in the business cycle. The principle resembles the adage, "Don't put all your eggs in one basket." Because the conglomerate is less risky, it pays a lower "risk premium" in capital markets—it buys the use of borrowed funds at a lower interest rate. Second, the cash flow patterns of the merging firms may differ, resulting in an improved cash flow match. Borrowing cash from a sister firm in an accounting transfer is likely to be less costly than obtaining cash in conventional capital markets.[131] Third, as even proponents recognize, a conglomerate may be able to

> allocate funds among its subdivisions in the fashion of a miniature capital market, with access to detailed information concerning the entities under its control and a wide range of incentives and control devices which are simply not available to investors in the external capital markets.[132]

By limiting conglomerate mergers, opponents argue, the proposed legislation would force the economy to forgo most of these benefits. Instead, firms would be pressed to reinvest in their own industries or to seek de novo entry into another industry. But, opponents argue, many U.S. industries involve maturing product markets with limited growth possibilities, or are markets in which foreign competitors have distinct advantages in the form of government subsidies or access to inexpensive labor.[133] Such markets, like other risky or cyclical markets, cannot be viewed by prudent managers as a desirable investment. De novo entry, on the other hand, "usually requires enormous capital and market development investments involving large risks which are particularly substantial for a large company accountable to hundreds of thousands of shareholders."[134]

Weston contends that, to the extent firms in industries that may be subject to de novo entry sell products priced on the basis of historical costs, including the cost of their fixed equipment, a de novo entrant will be at a distinct disadvantage because it must price on the basis of the much higher cost of new plant—replacement value rather than historical value. The cost of new capacity may be 50 percent higher than the cost of acquiring the same productive capacity through a corporate acquisition—essentially the purchase of used assets. Thus, conglomerate mergers stimulate competition by facilitating entry that might otherwise not occur. Moreover, mergers that produce increased efficiencies in production, distribution, or marketing, for example, may stimulate matching innovations by others, the very essence of competition with consequent benefits to society.[135]

The third category of efficiency gains that a conglomerate might realize stems from tax benefits. The most common advantage is the provision of positive earnings "to offset a tax loss carryforward. Not letting a tax loss carryforward go to waste is certainly a private efficiency; whether it is a social efficiency depends on one's opinion of the social utility of financing increased Government spending."[136] Other advantages may lie in the elimination of taxes on dividends or reinvested capital.[137]

Proponents contend that the legislation will result in minimal efficiency loss to society. They contend that the net economic benefits attributable to conglomerate firms are minimal and that any specific activities of conglomerate firms that may contribute to economic efficiency will not be blocked by the legislative proposals.

Proponents deny that modern-day mergers have the purpose or effect of revitalizing complacent management. In 1969, for example, at the peak of the merger wave, only 4 percent of acquired firms were reporting losses. One FTC study of mergers is cited to show that nearly 60 percent of the top managers of acquired firms involved in the study were retained.[138] According to advocates of conglomerate legislation, there is a tendency simply to layer new management on top of the management of acquired firms, thus leading to personality conflicts. They claim that, when fewer managers are used to achieve savings, too often the managers lack specialized ability. There is a limit, it is claimed, to the amount of complexity that such management can handle, and the fact that some firms voluntarily divest themselves of various assets suggests that some conglomerates are aware of these management problems. Insofar as certain firms strategically plan acquisitions to help themselves diversify, advocates of conglomerate legislation contend that there is no logical reason to believe that management of acquiring firms from declining industries are well qualified to manage growing firms in other markets. Proponents claim that conglomerates seek out well-managed, rather than trouble-ridden, companies.[139] Moreover, proponents argue, mergers tend to weaken rather than strengthen management. Not infrequently, a conglomerate merger will be followed by a mass exodus of managers who find the loss of autonomy and the more bureaucratic decision making of their new environment oppressive.

Proponents question the extent to which conglomerate mergers give rise to operating and capital economies. Some deny the existence of any economies whatsoever: "Since by its very nature the conglomerate firm is composed of functionally unrelated enterprises, it loses the advantage of specialization and the economies of scale pertaining thereto."[140] Most proponents, however, admit that limited efficiencies might plausibly occur in management, marketing and promotion, product development, and finance. But, they quickly add, "evidence confirming this possibility is nonetheless scant."[141]

Proponents also note the possibility that conglomeration will result in diseconomies, because of limitations on managerial span of control and reduced organizational flexibility. No matter how well structured an organization is, proponents argue, beyond a certain size its control becomes unwieldy.[142]

In addition, proponents argue that large firms limit to a narrow range their search for solutions to particular problems. One reason may be the complexity of communication within large firms. Another may be that benefits given to one division must be provided to other divisions as well.[143] Consequently, a large firm's response to a problem may be slower or less adequate than a small firm's. Examples include U.S. automakers' slow development of small cars and U.S. steel producers' delay in adopting the basic oxygen process.[144]

Why then, in the view of proponents, do conglomerate mergers occur? Too often, the merger "is to be explained in terms of opportunities for promotion profits, personal ambitions of industrial and financial Napoleons, and advantages of monopoly power."[145] Insofar as diversification is a motive for acquisitions, stockholders would be served equally well by selective investment in the stock shares of various firms.[146]

Proponents deny that mergers result in increased efficiency as reflected in profitability. For this, they rely on empirical studies which conclude that mergers do not, on the average, increase the profitability of the merging firms. Efficiency gains following acquisition would normally be reflected in increased profitability. Consequently, proponents argue, statistical evidence that mergers yield real efficiency gains is nonexistent.[147] Economies of scale are realized for the most part at the plant level, according to proponents, and thus there are few opportunities for significantly increased efficiency through conglomeration, particularly since many conglomerates permit acquired companies to operate essentially as before their acquisition.[148] Horizontal and vertical mergers may offer significant opportunities for increases in efficiency, but not conglomerate mergers.

Since conglomerates do not increase efficiency as measured by profitability, proponents insist that there would be no loss of efficiency if mergers involving firms above a certain threshold were banned, as proposed in the cited legislation. However, if firm managers can establish by a preponderance of evidence that a particular merger involving firms subject to the threshold will result in substantial efficiencies (or will substantially enhance competition), the legislation will not preclude merger. In addition, some legislative proposals permit a merger if the acquiring firm within one year spins off business units whose assets and revenues are equal to or greater than those of the acquired firm. Moreover, legislation would set firm guidelines and thus produce substantial savings in litigation costs both for the government and for the firms defending against antitrust actions.[149] There would be greater certainty in the antimerger law and businesses could plan for their future with much more confidence as to the antitrust consequences of their actions than is now true. A ready market would continue for the sale of businesses to firms below the threshold size (and to those above that size who could show that merger would result in substantial efficiencies or would substantially enhance competition), so entrepreneurs would not be discouraged from establishing new businesses in the hope that they could sell out at an appropriate time.[150]

Opponents deny the claim that empirical evidence shows that profitability figures do not demonstrate that firms realize increased efficiencies through conglomerate mergers. William F. Baxter states:

This line of argument is fallacious because it fails to account for the fact that acquiring firms typically have to pay premiums that amount, on average, to 15 to 20 percent above market price for the companies they acquire. Unless the mergers were efficiency producing, those premiums would represent enormous losses to the acquiring firm. Certainly economic research on this subject does not show that acquiring firms systematically sustain substantial losses. Efficiencies approximating those premiums must be achieved for the acquiring firm to break even.[151]

Richard A. Posner claims that empirical studies support the conclusion that:

acquired firms typically benefit from being acquired because their performance prior to merger was below average and was improved by the acquisition. This confirms that the corporate merger is indeed a device for transferring assets out of the hands of less competent managers and into the hands of more competent ones.[152]

Opponents of conglomerate legislation reply to arguments of proponents regarding the tax motivation for conglomerate mergers by noting that, if this is a problem, the solution is to change the tax laws or eliminate inflation by macroeconomic means, not tinker with the antimerger laws. As to contentions that mergers are motivated by the ambitions of managers for personal financial gain, opponents of legislation point out that studies of the behavior of stock prices for acquiring firms do not give managers the expectation of significant gains in the value of their stock holdings; it is the stock of the acquired firms that appreciates. As between the benefit of shareholders and that of managers, opponents point out that many people are competing for managerial jobs and, if shareholders' stock holdings decline, managers will be displaced by action of the board of directors or by takeover by another firm.[153]

To the claim that any efficiency gains from mergers should be disregarded as accruing only to certain stockholders or managers and not to the economy as a whole, opponents respond by asserting that, if a merger is good for the efficiency of the firms involved, it is certainly good for the economy. By contributing to a well-functioning market for capital assets, mergers put capital to its most productive use, oust less efficient managers, and contribute to efficiency and growth in the economy. Operating improvements are reflected in lower prices, better products, and increased output, thus increasing the level of living, and this benefits the economy quite aside from figures on profitability of the surviving firms.[154]

Opponents contend that, if some mergers lead to diseconomics of scale, the inefficient companies will soon be disciplined by the marketplace. Bork contends, moreover, that antitrust laws cannot appropriately permit federal courts to review and revise management judgments about efficiency. Imposing arbitrary limits on the size of firms, it is charged, will reduce the discipline of takeover threats and thereby reduce pressures for economic efficiency while impairing the operation of the market for capital assets. If restricting the operation of the capital market can be justified, then the restrictions should be extended to all segments of the market, for the total market is so interrelated that the operation of all parts of the market would be adversely affected by the restrictions. Since these limitations would make illegal what in fact may be procompetitive, litigation under the new statute would, according to opponents, in fact be a double waste.[155]

**Conglomerates and Inflation.** Proponents of measures to restrict conglomerate mergers argue that stagflation, defined as the simultaneous occurrence of high rates of both unemployment and inflation, is an important manifestation of the growth of multinational conglomerates in the American economy. In particular, they argue that firms in highly concentrated industries raise their prices even during recessions. Before the 1970s, firms in industries with low and medium concentration reduced their markups during recessionary periods, offsetting the behavior of firms in highly concentrated industries. As a result, the economy was not marked by stagflation: the inflation rate tended to vary inversely with the employment rate. Beginning in the late 1960s and 1970s, however, firms in industries with low and medium concentration began to increase price markups during recessions, just as firms in highly concentrated industries. No longer did different sectors of the economy contribute offsetting price effects; instead, all sectors contributed to stagflation. This result, proponents argue, can be traced directly to the growth of conglomerates: the conglomerates extended behavior of high-concentration sectors of the economy into those low-concentration sectors that traditionally had resisted stagflation.[156]

In response to the unusual economics implicit in this argument, opponents of the legislation point to studies which conclude that prices in concentrated industries do not differ systematically from prices in most other manufacturing industries. If any systematic relationship exists, it cannot be found in the data. The explanation is that most industries, regardless of level of concentration, are characterized by price inflexibility in the short run: in most industries prices are set by sellers, who because of uncertainty respond to changes in demand by initially adjusting inventory levels or output rather than price. Only in industries characterized by many small firms, where suppliers are price takers, do prices respond to demand in the short run.[157]

Were stagflation caused principally by high concentration, one would expect stagflation to have characterized the American economy of the early 1900s, following the first great merger wave, when most basic industries became highly concentrated. Instead, stagflation did not develop until the 1970s. Its principal causes appear to be not conglomerate growth, but rather such factors as changes in inflationary expectations and price shocks to the economy—such as the oil price increases by the Organization of Petroleum Exporting Countries (OPEC).

**Conglomerates and International Competition.** Proponents of measures to restrict conglomerate mergers rarely address its international ramifications. Opponents, on the other hand, frequently discuss the international effects, which they believe would be detrimental to the interests of the United States.

Opponents contend that proponents parochially view large corporations as competing solely in a domestic market, an economic Fortress America.[158] In fact, they claim, the relevant market is international. Until the end of the 1960s, U.S. export trade was only 3 or 4 percent of GNP. Over the last decade, however, of farm and factory production, the ratio of exports and imports to domestic goods production is closer to one-quarter—that is, one out of every four units produced in the United States. If any particular relevant market is viewed as international, concentration ratios drop markedly. One study calculated the average four-firm concentration ratio in seventy-five industries as slightly more than 50 percent. If the same industries were viewed in an international context, however, the concentration ratio declined to less than 25 percent.[159]

Other statistics reveal that U.S. corporations are vulnerable—and increasingly so—in international markets. Of the 502 corporations in the free world with sales exceeding $1 billion, 242, or slightly less than half, are based in the United States; and they are growing at a discernibly slower rate than their foreign counterparts. The share of international trade represented by U.S. corporations has also been declining—from 15.5 percent a decade ago to 11.5 percent in 1978. In contrast, Japan's share has increased from 8.3 percent to 11.5 percent over the same period.[160]

Opponents contend that the legislation will only hasten this decline by reducing the competitive potential of U.S. firms. Large, diversified firms, they argue, have the stability to withstand the ups and downs in inherently unstable international markets and are often the only organizations both willing and able to take the substantial risks entailed in doing business abroad. Senator Orrin G. Hatch (R-Utah) argues:

> We are at a time in our history when we should be doing all in our power to make it easier for our corporations to compete on an international basis. If American industry is to survive in the world market, and compete equally in the American market, it must have freedom to build size, diversity, and financial strength.[161]

A major problem seen by some opponents is that the United States would be unable to meet emerging global realities in trade because the federal government would block requisite mergers. Irving Shapiro, then chairman of du Pont, argued that we already suffer from restrictive antitrust laws that hold American companies to tougher standards overseas than competing foreign firms face and that the pending legislation would only aggravate the problem.[162] In contrast, opponents claim that Canada, the Common Market nations, and Japan have bolstered their competitive stance in international markets by encouraging mergers and cartels. In Japan, for example, the government has even forced mergers. Similarly, centrally planned economies are becoming more important factors in world trade.[163]

Opponents also argue that the proposal of the FTC's Bureau of Competition would discourage foreign investment in the United States, since foreign firms would be subject to its terms. One result would be fewer jobs domestically. Another result would be the possibility of diplomatic dispute: foreign governments could be expected to resent the legislation as an example of American protectionist policy. Other proposals, however, contain no provisions to block acquisitions of U.S. firms by foreign companies. Thus, under those proposals, though U.S. companies would be stopped from buying up other companies at home if the acquisitions would breach the limits set in the bills, foreign investors would be free to acquire almost as many firms as they wished. This would drive domestic firms to acquire foreign firms, with an accompanying drain on U.S. funds and the export of jobs from this country.[164]

Milton D. Stewart, former chief counsel for advocacy at the Small Business Administration, argues, however, that corporate size is not necessary to compete in the international marketplace. He contends, first, that bigger is better only to the point at which peak economy of scale is reached and, second, that much of American industry has reached or passed that point already.[165] Proponents insist that only when a merger will produce significant economies of scale or synergies could the competitive posture of the companies be improved by merger, and the principal legislative proposals permit mergers if they will produce substantial efficiencies or substantially enhance competition.

## Social and Political Issues

**Conglomerates and the Antitrust Tradition.** Proponents of measures to restrict conglomerate mergers contend that their proposals are consistent with the social and political values that underlie the antitrust laws. Proponents point to the legislative debates and historical context surrounding passage of the Sherman, Clayton, and Celler-Kefauver Acts. Although Congress employed economic concepts in regulating the business environment, proponents contend that the underlying congressional intention was to affect economic decision making in a manner that would preserve the social and political fabric of the nation. Alfred Dougherty, for example, points to historian Richard Hofstadter's description of the Progressive Era, a critical period in the development of antitrust policy. Hofstadter wrote:

> The progressive case against business organizations was not confined to economic considerations. . . . At bottom, the central fear was fear of power and the greater the strength of an organized interest the greater anxiety it aroused. Hence, it was the trusts, the investment banking houses, the interlocking directorates, the swollen private fortunes that were most criticized.[166]

Dougherty notes that similar fears were expressed by Senator Sherman in 1890 in connection with the adoption of the Sherman Antitrust Act and by Senator Estes Kefauver (D-Tenn.) during the debates preceding adoption of the Celler-Kefauver Act in 1950. Proponents cite the Supreme Court's reference in its *Brown Shoe* decision to congressional concern for "accelerated concentration of economic power on economic grounds, but also the threat to other values a trend toward concentration was thought to pose."[167] Similarly, Judge Learned Hand in the *Alcoa* case referred to noneconomic as well as economic bases for "the belief that great industrial consolidations are inherently undesirable."[168] Michael Pertschuk, former chairman and now member of the Federal Trade Commission, argues that large conglomerate mergers should be banned because they increase the participating firms' power at the expense of smaller and less organized groups and at the expense of the individual. Thus, many proponents of measures to restrict conglomerate mergers primarily justify adoption of such measures by the need to attain political and social objectives rather than on the basis of concern for economic concentration or market efficiency.[169]

Opponents admit that current antitrust laws reflect concerns over the social and political effects of large firms. They contend, however, that Congress deliberately chose to achieve its social and political objectives by enacting economic standards to preserve competition in the marketplace, rather than by enacting standards of legality based on social or political performance. This, it is claimed, is reflected in recent decisions of the Supreme Court that reject arguments based directly on social and political concerns. Opponents cite Turner, who argues that the social purpose to preserve small business, for example, has never been translated into rules banning conduct that is not anticompetitive on some other basis, and that Congress has not given the courts and the FTC a mandate to campaign against superconcentration without evidence of harm to competition.[170] Ira M. Millstein, a former chairman of the American Bar Association section on antitrust law, notes that Congress in enacting antitrust legislation chose to achieve its social and political objectives not by enacting a standard of legality based on social or political performance, but rather by enacting laws to keep the market free from potentially anticompetitive mergers, monopolies, and unreasonable restraints of trade.[171]

Unless competition is threatened, opponents argue, the mere assertion of adverse social impact has never provided a basis for antitrust attack. They claim that, viewed against this background, the proposed legislation departs significantly from antitrust tradition. Rather than protecting competition, the legislation seeks to achieve social and political objectives directly, based on the unproven assumption that corporate size adversely affects social and political interests. Were the legislation to remain within the antitrust tradition of protecting social and political values by preserving competition, it would be unnecessary, because existing antitrust laws already impose extraordinarily—perhaps excessively—stringent standards in measuring the anticompetitive effect of mergers.[172]

Proponents of the legislation also contend that conglomerate mergers threaten the fundamental principles of Jeffersonian democracy, principles that provided the basis for the later economic populism from which antitrust sprouted.[173] Arguing against concentration of economic power, Jefferson urged the adoption of measures to disperse decision-making authority widely throughout society. The Jeffersonian symbols were

> small, local, responsible, and individually-owned enterprises contrasted with large, politically irresponsible, absentee-owned, and possibly corrupt giants capable of crushing smaller businessmen and individuals and of subverting democratic government. In the Jeffersonian world, economic power is held in check; the virtues of sturdy independent entrepreneurship are maximized; and political democracy is thought easiest to preserve.[174]

Proponents argue that giant firms represent enormous aggregations of economic resources. Giant firms seem like "private governments, subject to few external constraints, and able to bring considerable resources to bear on any issue of their choosing. Management is largely self-perpetuating, and control passes from one person to another with few of the cleansing attributes of public accountability."[175]

Opponents regard the Jeffersonian vision as plainly inappropriate to modern society. Certainly the ideal is a cherished political heritage, but "to wrench it from the context of an agrarian economy of the 18th and early 19th centuries and apply it dogmatically" to the present economic and political order overlooks the changes that have occurred in the interim.[176] The badges of power in Jefferson's Virginia consisted of land holdings and ownership of shops. Today's society is technologically more complex; economic markets and political forces span the globe; and the power of business interests is now offset by labor unions, consumer groups, and other countervailing forces.[177] Bork, for example, notes that the vocabulary of the tradition cited by proponents is an attractive one but that the underlying conceptions are a "jumble of half-digested notions and mythologies" and, insofar as it can be said that there is a theory behind the tradition, it is that efficiency should sometimes be curbed because of the social and political health supposedly engendered by the preservation of independent small businesses.[178]

**Conglomerates and Political Influence.** Proponents of measures to restrict conglomerate mergers believe that such mergers have two effects that confer disproportionate political influence on the resulting firm: mergers necessarily reduce the number of independent political voices; and mergers produce larger, more diversified firms, which in the view of proponents are able to court special political advantage. Bain argues that such firms have disproportionate influence on political elections through campaign contributions, on legislation through well-financed lobbies, and on government regulatory policies through their success in staffing regulatory agencies with persons sympathetic to their interests.[179] Walter Adams contends that recent events demonstrate that conglomerate power "conveys unique access to political power and the opportunity to transform the state into an instrument of privilege creation and protection."[180] The eventual result, proponents fear, will be the political disenchantment of the citizenry; new regulatory apparatus to control conglomerate activity; and, at the extreme, the development of socialism or fascism.

Opponents believe that the claims of adverse political consequences are unsupported by credible evidence. Rather, they observe, other political interests wield more political power than big business, and big business has consistently lost major political battles in recent years. To predict that conglomeration is leading society toward fascism and socialism is simply a hysterical response.

*Reduction of political voices.* Proponents regard diverse and decentralized political power as fundamental to the American system: our democracy assumes a "multiplicity of tongues" competing in the political marketplace. A conglomerate merger, however, reduces the number of independent political voices and concentrates political strength in the merged firm. Further, the merger is likely to reduce political diversity: the formerly independent firms were likely to have had divergent interests and to have expressed different views on political issues. In contrast, the merged firm presents a single position on political issues.[181]

Opponents claim that numerous other interest groups counterbalance the political power of large firms. Among the most prominent are consumer groups, farm groups, small business groups, and labor unions, all with independent political strength and all capable of deploying their own power bases to counteract any untoward corporate advances. Jesse Markham, for example, argues that in "the Boston area where I live we feel the power of Mr. [Frank] Fitzsimmon's Teamsters union to virtually close down the economy much more than that of the president of the Textron Corp. headquartered in nearby Providence, R.I."[182]

Opponents argue that, even if the merged firm may hold more political power than its formerly independent parts, nonetheless, overall political strength has been reduced. The "mere fact that a very large corporation has more influence than a small corporation does not mean that it is proportionately more powerful," since a "group of small corporations may have much more influence than a single large corporation which is as large or larger than the sum of the small organizations."[183]

In rejoinder, proponents argue that a group of individual firms is less likely to hold together in a commitment to a political objective than is a single large firm.[184]

*Political advantage of large firms.* Proponents claim that large and diversified firms have special advantages in political advocacy. It is argued, for example, that "the political and social power held by executives of large conglomerate enterprises is significant. Executives of large corporations have the power . . . to affect public opinion on important political issues."[185] Proponents point to three theoretical considerations in explaining why large corporations are especially advantaged. First, large firms are less concerned about the "free rider" problem—that they may bear the burden and cost of obtaining political relief, but their competition will share the benefit. Large, diversified firms may also have the ability to mobilize diverse economic forces from different industries toward a common political objective. Finally, there may be scale economies in certain kinds of political activities.[186] Large firms, it is claimed, can meet the threshold of expenditures required for attaining effective political influence while small firms cannot.

In support of these theoretical considerations, proponents point out that larger firms are more likely to be represented by permanent professional lobbying organizations than smaller firms; that larger firms may be more effective in the lobbying process because of their greater use of corporate executives; and that larger firms are able to mobilize greater numbers of shareholders, dealers, and suppliers in support of their political interests.[187] Further, large organizations are more likely to be heard by decision makers. Proponents cite the late Senator Phillip Hart's statement: "When a major corporation from a state wants to discuss something with its political representatives you can be sure it will be heard. When that same company operates in thirty states it will be heard thirty times."[188] William S. Comanor contends that, in smaller communities, large corporations are perceived as much like local governments. They respond to local authorities as equals rather than as citizens subject to the law, and matters such as local taxation become subjects of negotiation with such firms.[189]

Proponents are especially troubled by the use of corporate political action committees (PACs) to influence the outcome of congressional races through campaign contributions. Among contested races in 1978, 82 percent of the House winners and 85 percent of the Senate winners were the bigger spenders. Admitting that the relationship between campaign contributions and political favoritism has always been murky, proponents nonetheless claim that "larger firms may be better able (or more apt) to coordinate contributions than smaller firms."[190] Among the *Fortune* 1,000 industrial firms, proponents argue, firm size is correlated with the existence of PACs:[191]

| *Rank of Firms* | *Number of PACs* | *Percentage of Firms with PACs* |
|---|---|---|
| 1st 100 | 63 | 63 |
| 1st 200 | 111 | 55 |
| 1st 500 | 166 | 33 |
| 1st 1,000 | 198 | 20 |

Opponents of the legislation contend that the alleged political advantages of large firms are unsupported by credible evidence. Only recently have scholars undertaken rigorous empirical research into the political consequences of large mergers. Some of these studies attempt to determine if there is a correlation between absolute firm size and disproportionate political influence, but many of the firms involved may be single-industry firms rather than conglomerates. Firms that do become more diverse through conglomerate acquisitions, it is argued, will find that the interests of the members of the corporate family may conflict rather than coincide.[192] In such instances, the firms may avoid attempts to influence legislation or they may leave each member of the corporate family to deal with its own concerns. In the latter case, diversity of opinion is clearly preserved.

The "evidence" advanced to show adverse consequences, opponents claim, consists of isolated anecdotes, journalistic reports, vague threats, and "scatological studies." Such evidence does not "manifest even a scintilla of conceptual and methodological analytical rigor which would justify designating [it] as scholarly, let alone scientific."[193] Opponents contend that, in the absence of rigorous analysis, general statements regarding adverse political consequences of mergers cannot be justified. To the extent that the legislative battle is fought with anecdotes, opponents offer anecdotes of their own to support their claim that the political power of large corporations has declined steadily over the last decade. Regulations that are harmful to business have increasingly been imposed: pollution, worker and consumer safety, and discrimination provide examples.[194] At the same time, those regulatory regimes that favor large business are being repealed: airlines and trucking offer examples. Still other regulations favor small businesses over large, suggesting that political influence accrues to the small businessman. It is argued, for example, that oil and gas regulations issued over the last thirty years have "regularly advantaged the smaller petroleum companies, and disadvantaged or at least brought no gain for the really big companies.[195] Similarly, in the television industry, political clout resides not in the networks, but in network affiliates and in independent stations. In the banking industry, smaller local banks enjoy favorable regulations limiting the expansion of large branch banks and bank holding companies. In the automobile industry, legislative enactments and judicial interpretations have protected dealers at the same time that manufacturers have been subjected to intrusive and stringent safety and pollution regulations.[196]

Besides anecdotal evidence, opponents also point to several empirical studies relating corporate size to political favor. One found that there is no significant correlation between the maximum corporate income tax in each state and the number of major corporations headquartered there. Another study found no significant correlation between the number of major corporations headquartered in each state and the number of special favors for businesses, as defined in a publication of the Council of State Governments. Internationally, there is no significant correlation between the corporate income tax rate in a sample of countries and the measure of corporate dominance in those countries.[197]

Opponents cite scholars who have surveyed the various empirical studies and concluded that the studies show no evidence that large firms spend a disproportionate amount on political activities or that they have disproportionate power. Edwin Epstein contends, moreover, that we do not have even minimally reliable measures of corporate political and social power.[198] Moreover, smaller firms effectively exert influence through trade associations and other organizations, quite apart from their resources and efforts devoted to direct attempts to exert political influence.

Opponents also question the relation between campaign contributions and firm size: of the 812 corporations that had registered PACs with the Federal Election Commission before the 1978 election, fewer than half (334, or 41 percent) were included on any of the 1978 *Fortune* lists of the 1,300 largest U.S. firms in seven industry classifications. Admitting that PAC frequency is correlated with firm size, opponents point out that a substantial number of even the largest firms have not created PACs. Furthermore, conglomerate mergers reduce the political power of corporate PACs: under the Federal Election Campaign Act of 1976, all PACs affiliated with a single conglomerate parent are subject to a single contribution limit. Therefore, the "more mergers, paradoxically, the fewer potential PACs."[199]

*Ultimate political vision.* As conglomerates grow, some proponents contend, citizens will increasingly believe themselves unable to influence political decision making. They "may conclude that their futures are being determined by remote forces" and "may simply lose faith in our economy and grow increasingly frustrated about their perceived powerlessness in the face of very large organizations."[200] Alternatively, the public may demand increased government control of large corporate enterprises, giving rise to the danger that society will move away from relatively free enterprise toward a concentrated, tightly controlled economy. Senator Kennedy has observed that "where business overwhelms the public by its size, a natural response of Government is to regulate it or even nationalize it. Many western democracies have chosen the latter route."[201] Some proponents see the fulfillment of this prediction in the statement of former Secretary of War Kenneth C. Royall's description of cartelization and concentration of industry in Germany:

> Germany under the Nazi set-up built up a great series of industrial monopolies in the fields of rubber, coal, and other materials. The monopolies soon got control of Germany, brought Hitler to power and forced virtually the whole world into war.[202]

Opponents of the legislation regard such fears as hysterical reactions without basis. The purported link between German cartels and the rise of Nazism is most easily calmed: history reveals no link at all. In general, German corporations in the 1920s supported parties in the middle of the political spectrum rather than the Nazis on the right or the Communists on the left. It is doubtful that corporate interests would have supported the Nazis: the Nazis, or National Socialists, wished to nationalize much of German industry. The rise of Nazism was caused not by large corporations, but rather by economic depression, accompanied by mass unemployment and economic destitution. Indeed, corporate power was relatively unconcentrated in Germany during the 1920s and 1930s, compared with the rest of Europe. France was more cartelized than Germany, and industry was more concentrated in Belgium, the Netherlands, Switzerland, and the Scandinavian countries than in Germany.[203]

In the view of opponents, the argument that large corporations require a large government to regulate them, while on its face attractive, is incorrect, since it "clearly takes more regulators to deal with an industry of 100,000 small shopkeepers than to deal with an industry with one large central organization."[204]

**Conglomerates and Social Harm.** Proponents of the legislation contend that conglomerates threaten numerous social interests. One source of the threat is the discretionary power wielded by large firms. A second source is the physical and psychological distance between the conglomerate decision maker and those he is affecting; the result may be community breakdown, plant closings, and harm to labor. In the view of opponents, on the other hand, the marketplace and government regulations together are so constraining that large firms have little discretionary power. Opponents admit that communities break down and plants close, but they argue that the link between such problems and size or conglomeration is unsubstantiated. Opponents ask what standard is to govern social good, for conglomeration brings a series of benefits to consumers, communities, and workers.

*Discretionary power.* Proponents of the legislation claim that large firms have social effects because they possess discretionary power, defined as "a range of business choice not dictated by or fully predictable from pure profit maximizing behavior."[205] If a particular business decision has little or no effect on profits or only an uncertain effect, a firm has discretion in choosing between available alternatives. Because the firm's decision is not constrained by profit maximization, the decision "may be made for any reason at all—or for no reason. Under such circumstances the choice may be made on the basis of a desire to produce social benefits. Or it may be based on whim, personal prejudice, or even malevolence."[206]

Social choices subject to the exercise of discretionary authority include plant and office location, charitable contributions, hiring and promotion decisions, and choice of technology. Because such choices are rarely dictated solely by profit maximization, proponents argue, firms may base their decisions on any of a wide range of other factors, including college or family ties, religious affiliation, accents, sex, or race. Such choices clearly have the power to affect large numbers of persons, communities, and sources of capital and technology.[207]

Proponents admit that the mere existence of discretionary power is not in itself harmful: Any purchaser from a perfectly competitive industry has complete discretion in choosing his particular supplier. Rather, discretionary power poses a threat only when it becomes concentrated in relatively few hands. Proponents believe that dispersion of power "protects us from the danger that the prejudices of one firm, or possibly even of one person, will significantly reduce the welfare of many."[208]

Some advocates of legislation restricting conglomerate mergers maintain that the argument discussed above—that it is undesirable to allow conglomeration to limit the number of decision makers—is not really limited to areas of discretionary power. In this view, the market will not reach optimal results unless some competitior devises a better strategy or better product, for example, and forces its rivals to follow its lead or originate even better strategies or products. Proponents insist that better strategies and better products are more likely, on average, when there are many independent decision makers rather than when all decision making in an industry is controlled by a small number of firms. The more decision makers there are, the more likely that at least one of them will hit on the optimal strategy or product, at which point the market will force the others to follow.

Opponents of measures to restrict conglomerate mergers and acquisitions question whether in fact large firms actually possess discretionary power. They point to a series of governmental and nongovernmental pressures that constrain large corporations, including conglomerates, in their decision-making processes. These include laws that ensure accountability to stockholders and the disclosure of relevant financial information to the investing public generally, competition in the marketplace from other strong firms including foreign manufacturers, public opinion, the media, pressure from various interest groups including stockholders, and finally a wide array of government regulations adopted to make certain that corporations operate in the public interest.[209]

To the extent that large corporations have any discretionary power, opponents claim, that power has been exercised in socially responsive ways. Opponents cite evidence showing a strong and positive correlation between firm size and corporate social responsibility. For example, a recent study commissioned by the Royal Commission on Corporate Concentration in Canada found that: "As the size of the firms increases (either on the basis of annual growth revenues or total number of employees) the levels of awareness/recognition, analysis/planning and response to corporate social involvement increases." Similar patterns seem to exist in France and Germany. Although no similar data are available for the United States, opponents point to several studies indicating a trend toward more corporate attention to social performance.[210]

Some opponents of conglomerate legislation contend that, by pursuing the firm's interest in maximizing profits, firm managers frequently promote the welfare of society more effectively than if they rely on vague social goals in decision making. Indeed, they ask, can self-selected individuals, such as the proponents of conglomerate legislation, decide for us what the social interest really is? If all business decisions must be made in the "social interest," according to Markham, this would bog down the entire economy.[211]

> The net effect of prohibiting conglomerate mergers, therefore, is more likely to be a decrease in growth and investment, with corresponding decreases in employment or in the rate of rise of productivity and wage rates. Workers and communities would suffer as new and improved job opportunities were lessened.[212]

*Community effect.* Proponents contend that conglomerate mergers contribute to the breakdown of communities by virtue of absentee ownership. When a local firm is absorbed into a conglomerate based elsewhere, local ownership and control cease. Productive assets, upon which community livelihood and survival depend, fall into the control of absent individuals without obligation or accountability at the local level. Discretionary policy decisions by corporations that affect the community, formerly made locally, are now made by distant headquarters, which may discount or be unaware of local community concerns. Services formerly performed locally, such as finance, legal services, and accounting, may be transferred elsewhere.[213]

Proponents cite the observations of Justice William O. Douglas on the community erosion that flows from absentee control:

> Local leadership is diluted. He who was a leader in the village becomes dependent on outsiders for his action and policy. Clerks responsible to a superior in a distant place take the place of resident proprietors beholden to no one. These are the prices which the Nation pays for the almost ceaseless growth in bigness on the part of industry.[214]

Opponents characterize the community breakdown argument as "self-serving cant propagated mainly by inefficient local businessmen who fear being taken over by, or having to compete against, more efficient firms."[215] Further, mergers often have the effect of diffusing political and social power at the local level. Oftentimes, particularly in old and small communities with business firms dependent upon the locale, business leadership may control the community.

Contrary to the romanticism about the advantage to the community from locally controlled businesses, opponents maintain, homegrown business leaders not uncommonly have been baronial in their styles and they are frequently anticosmopolitan and antidevelopment, thus leaving their communities less advanced socially and with less per capita income than they might otherwise enjoy. In contrast, absentee national operations have tended toward noninvolvement on the local level. Consequently, merger activity may reduce the social and political control exercised by local business executives and diffuse control among the local citizenry.[216]

Irving Shapiro maintains that whether or not business decisions adversely affect local communities has everything to do with size and nothing to do with antitrust and conglomerate mergers. Any large company with more than one plant that has any semblance of decentralized management is putting some business decisions in absentee hands.[217]

*Plant closings.* Proponents point to plant closings as an especially detrimental community effect arising from conglomerate mergers. They believe that a large corporation will worry less than a locally run enterprise about making a decision to close facilities. As a result, proponents fear, "an enterprise that could have remained economically viable will be lost because of a management decision made elsewhere."[218]

In the view of opponents, the arguments about plant closings rest on isolated anecdotes. Opponents admit that plant closings do occur and that such closings harm community interests. Plants are also closed, however, by small companies or by companies uninvolved in merger activity. Zenith, for example, although not involved in any merger, recently closed its assembly facilities in Sioux City, Iowa. Similarly, Goodyear and Firestone closed automobile tire facilities in Akron, Ohio. Opponents claim that "no one has offered any data to show that plant closings occur with disproportionate frequency after conglomerate mergers. If they do not occur with disproportionate frequency, then the issue of plant closings is totally irrelevant" to the legislative debate.[219]

George J. Benston maintains that there is no evidence in general that local firms would choose to maintain rather than close a plant that is not operating successfully. Moreover, according to Benston, a small, single-industry firm is more likely to go bankrupt with consequent adverse effects on the community than is a larger diversified enterprise, and the U.S. Chamber of Commerce argues that plant closings are a small business problem.[220] Shapiro maintains that his firm, du Pont, has gone the extra mile to put capital into communities to create or preserve jobs that would otherwise disappear, and du Pont has salvaged and rebuilt declining plants when not once was this the low-cost option. [221]

Although a plant closing may prove painful to the affected community, opponents contend that plant closings are often desirable under the competitive process, holding cost and prices as low as possible. When an ineffecient plant is closed in one community, the normal reason is that the firm expects to employ resources more productively elsewhere, and for every plant closed another may open elsewhere. The nation as a whole gains from the shift.[222]

*Threats to labor.* Proponents contend that conglomeration harms labor relations. Workers must seriously consider the brooding threat of a plant shutdown, particularly unless they make bargaining concessions. Against this background, the conglomerate may demand new work standards or contract settlements deviating from accepted community standards. The conglomerate is less likely to be as flexible as the former local owner, because absentee managers are insulated from the decision-making process, because the conglomerate may benefit from standardization, and because the conglomerate may be better able to withstand a prolonged strike than a local firm.

Employees suffer personal trauma as well. Those top managers who formerly controlled the local firm suffer career damage. Young executives find career paths limited. Other workers fear elimination of jobs through consolidations of administrative and operating segments. As worker unhappiness increases, productivity and efficiency decline.[223]

Opponents note that such arguments are reconstituted versions of the plant closing, community effect, and cross-subsidization claims raised by proponents in other contexts. The reconstituted versions suffer from the same defects as the originals. The supposition that a plant under conglomerate ownership is especially susceptible to closing appears unfounded. Regardless of its owner, an unprofitable plant will be closed, and a profitable plant will remain open. As to the threat of renegotiated standards, the claim again raises a conflict between the interests of the affected workers and the interests of consumers through increased production, lower prices, better quality, and a healthy economy. Work standards will normally be changed for reasons of efficiency, desirable within the competitive process. Finally, as to the conglomerate's special ability to withstand a labor dispute, the argument recalls the threat of cross-subsidization and deep-pocket financing. In general, such practices prove economically irrational and will seldom be undertaken by a business firm.

Opponents also note that large labor unions fully offset any advantage that a large company might otherwise have in negotiations. One study notes that it is hometown firms that are often antiunion and favor loose labor markets.[224]

Opponents maintain, moreover, that it is plant size rather than overall firm size that primarily affects worker morale. Since this problem obtains with single-industry firms, it is not a problem peculiar to conglomerates. While it is true that worker satisfaction decreases somewhat with increased plant size, workers in larger establishments are better paid and employers find other ways to compensate for the problem of plant size. Indeed, according to Benston, diversification benefits employees by providing them opportunities for advancement, training, and relocation. Employees can change jobs without changing companies, and employees benefit from greater stability through diversification.[225]

## Administrative Issues Involved in Proposals to Amend the Antitrust Laws

Opponents contend that the conglomerate merger legislation, if passed, would be plagued by administrative difficulties. In their view, the legislation would lead to enormously complex and possibly unmanageable litigation and would create uncertainties both in the business world and in the courts for some time to come.

Opponents object that parties to a merger often could not conclusively determine whether the legislation applies to them. S. 600, the Concentrated Industries Act, the FTC plan, and the Justice Department plan all establish dollar thresholds based on assets or sales, and the Hart plan is triggered by average profits exceeding a certain percentage. Yet the proposals offer no guidance in defining such terms, or in detailing the underlying accounting assumptions to be employed in determining profits. Opponents fear both conceptual and practical evaluation problems. Most critically, the proposals do "not indicate whether a firm's assets or sales are to be measured on a net or on a gross basis; whether a firm's assets or sales are to include the assets or sales of its subsidiaries; or whether a firm's assets or sales are to be measured on the basis of a firm's total assets or sales, including any foreign based assets or sales."[226] For example, assets might alternatively be measured in terms of salvage value, book value, or replacement cost. It is unclear from the proposals whether depreciation may be taken into account—and if it may, which lifespans are appropriate and which acceleration methods permissible. The proposals also overlook the variety of legal arrangements through which firms obtain use of assets, including long-term leases and leases with a purchase option. Such definitional shortcomings raise the specter that every merger "could become the functional equivalent of a utility commission rate case with testimony and countertestimony over the value of the 'rate base.' "[227]

Similar problems are created by the use of a "market share" criterion in S. 600, the Hart plan, the Concentrated Industries Act, and the Justice Department plan. Whether a firm has, say, a 20 percent market share depends on the definition of the market. Yet the task of market definition is normally fraught with ambiguity. Statutory reliance on a market share criterion will necessarily cause uncertainty and will likely provoke costly litigation. Furthermore, even if the market can be defined, parties to a merger will rarely have precise market share data: published sales figures are rarely broken out by market lines applicable for antitrust purposes. If, as is likely, a firm were forced to obtain detailed private sales figures of competitors in order to determine its market share, it might run afoul of other antitrust provisions.

Such uncertainties could be minimized if parties to a merger were able to obtain from enforcement authorities a binding determination of whether the legislation applied in their particular instance. Not all of the legislative proposals, however, provide for such determinations. Even if such determinations were available, however, opponents fear that enforcement authorities would resolve ambiguity so as to tailor their decision to the political fashion of the moment.

Opponents also question the advisability of legislating specific dollar thresholds in the first place. In their view, the selection of thresholds is necessarily arbitrary. "It is, indeed, inescapable that a bill, motivated as this one is by objectives which are abstract and imperceptible if not vacuous and nonexistent, must use arbitrary bright-line boundaries rather than functional criteria . . . which tell . . . the courts to employ the objective that the legislature was pursuing."[228] Opponents note, for example, that the legislation applies to all industries without differentiation, even though any specific dollar value represents different things to different industries. Furthermore, the use of specific dollar thresholds enables firms to evade the legislation. A firm within the range of a particular threshold could push itself above or below through a variety of maneuvers, including changes in depreciation schedules, inventory evaluation methods, timetables for replacing equipment and facilities, and transportation methods.

Firms approaching the thresholds in the proposals would have incentive to shy away from new product development and reduce their competitive efforts in order to remain below the threshold. Much energy and effort would be wasted on uneconomic evasion activities. Thus, the legislation would reduce efficiency and curtail competition, when the opposite prescription is required for consumer welfare. No-fault antimerger legislation, moreover, would substitute affirmative regulatory intervention in the economy for the discipline of the invisible hand of the marketplace at a time when economic regulatory approaches generally have been substantially discredited. Opponents maintain that it would be better to change the economic and financial environment that make mergers attractive than to pass laws that will create economic distortions without addressing the fundamental problems involved.[229]

Opponents note that the dollar thresholds in most of the proposals are not indexed to take account of inflation. Consequently, each year more and more firms will be brought within the legislations' terms, and more firms will engage in distortionary maneuvers.[230] Most bills also fail to specify whether acquisitions by foreign companies fall within the reach of the statute. If they do not, the legislation would concede a great advantage to foreign competitors. If such acquisitions are within the reach of the statute, serious problems of international relations may be raised by actions of the FTC and the Justice Department against foreign firms.

Opponents criticize the legislative proposals that would establish numerical thresholds so that firms exceeding these thresholds would be in violation of the law regardless of the justification for their actions or, as in some proposals, those firms exceeding stated thresholds would violate the law unless they can prove to the court's satisfaction that the merger or acquisition will substantially enhance competition and promote economic efficiency or that they will divest assets to bring the firm below the threshold cited in the proposal. Opponents maintain that the traditional concept of fair play in U.S. courts requires that those opposing a merger or acquisition prove a violation of the law, either that the merger or acquisition will substantially lessen competition or that it will tend to create a monopoly.

Opponents maintain, for reasons outlined earlier in this analysis, that proponents have not made out a case for reversing the traditional burden of proving that a merger or acquisition will substantially lessen competition or tend to create a monopoly. Moreover, even if a change in the burden of proof is to be made, the legislative proposals contain the wrong prescription.

Opponents argue that proving the two affirmative defenses of substantial efficiencies or enhanced competition presents an almost impossible burden. The proposals tell those who seek to acquire other firms that they are guilty until they prove themselves innocent.[231] "How does one prove, for example, that one manager is better than another, and further, that a contemplated change of management effected through a merger will substantially enhance competition? How does one prove that increased economies of scale or increased specialization will result from a given transaction, and further, that such changes will substantially enhance competition?[232] Unfortunately, the economic bases for efficiency gains are difficult to establish before the event and especially difficult within the adversary arena of the courts. The cost of such a law in confusion and litigation would, according to opponents, be enormous.[233]

The third affirmative defense, known as "cap and spinoff," is attacked on several grounds. First, it is often difficult to find a suitable buyer for the stock or assets to be divested because timing is crucial.[234] Second, assets are often commingled, and their unscrambling is difficult. Most critically, the provision conflicts with the goals underlying the legislation. A large firm divesting itself of a going concern would most likely sell it to another large firm; few other purchasers have adequate cash or securities to buy an entire going concern. The purchaser, however, would then have to divest itself of another going concern, and so forth. The cap-and-spinoff provision, then, will generate numerous unnecessary transactions. To the extent that conglomerate mergers cause political and social disruption, the effects will be multiplied. Such chain reactions would be avoided if the legislation permitted divestiture through liquidation rather than through spinoff of a going concern—but other problems would arise. In particular, competition would be reduced in the market in which the liquidated firm had operated.

Opponents object to the proposal to write actual potential competition theory into the antitrust statutes. They argue that the theory is so extreme and unsatisfactory that no court has endorsed it and, if its adoption is coupled with a reduced burden of proof as is proposed, it is subject to the same objections to shifting the burden of proof that are cited above.

Proponents respond to the foregoing criticisms of the legislative proposals by asserting that the burden of proof imposed on those challenging conglomerate mergers and acquisitions is too great and that the benefits of decentralized decision making and the protection of the political and social values cited earlier cannot be attained without a restructuring of the antimerger laws. Proponents note that their aim is to block very large conglomerate mergers. That aim is not undermined if numerous firms straddling the statutory thresholds manage to evade the force of the legislation through creative asset valuation or operational changes: "in most endeavors we let the small ones get away." The thresholds are such that the conglomerate mergers that pose true threats will clearly and unambiguously fall within the statutory net.

Proponents view the affirmative defense provisions as necessary for good public policy. Although larger mergers are viewed as objectionable, certain particular mergers possess such unusual benefits that, on balance, the objections are more than outweighed. The affirmative defense provisions will permit the courts and enforcement authorities to recognize the limited number of mergers that result in net public benefit.

Mergers are now subject to government regulation under current antitrust law, but that law is imprecise and difficult to administer. Publishing firm guidelines about the illegality of mergers will provide certainty in business planning and thus save much time and litigation expense. When appropriate benefits to competition or efficiency can be shown, large conglomerate mergers will be permitted.[235]

# 5

## CONCLUSION

The debate over measures to restrict conglomerate mergers is, according to some scholars, analytically elusive because of uncertainties about various data employed in the debate. Issues such as firm size, industrial concentration, and individual firm performance in terms of prices and so forth cannot be satisfactorily resolved, according to scholars, until better data are available. Some opponents of measures to restrict conglomerate mergers argue that the lack of more precise data is sufficient reason to postpone consideration of the radical step of adopting a massive new standard for regulating mergers and acquisitions, a standard that may have unforeseen consequences. Proponents contend, on the other hand, that opponents are inconsistent for, without a major change in antimerger law, parties will continue to litigate conglomerate merger cases under the current imprecise statutory antimerger standards using the same imprecise factual data that have made debate over measures to restrict conglomerate mergers less than satisfactory. Many opponents maintain that the data are precise enough now to demonstrate that we do not need a more restrictive antimerger policy.

The continuing debate over antimerger policy may be sharpened by a number of developments in the ensuing months. William Baxter, the new assistant attorney general for the Antitrust Division, promises to rewrite that division's merger guidelines, presumably to highlight, in part, a less restrictive stance on conglomerate mergers. The Federal Trade Commission has long contended that business reporting based on a single set of results for diversified firms has masked the performance of conglomerates in various lines and the degree of industrial concentration in various industries, because these reports are not broken out by product line. The first results of line-of-business reporting are now being compiled by the FTC. Some scholars expect these reports and the development of new methods of interpreting data to bring us closer to the facts that are relevant to antimerger policy. A decision of the FTC favorable to the actual potential competition doctrine will be reviewed by the U.S. Court of Appeals, and its decision may shed more light on whether this theory will fly, absent legislative endorsement. Representative Peter W. Rodino, Jr. (D-N.J.), chairman of the Judiciary Committee and its Subcommittee on Antitrust and Commercial Law, expects to hold hearings later this year on why U.S. industry is falling behind foreign competition. These hearings may focus on companies that are busy acquiring other firms rather than using the resources devoted to acquisitions for research and development and attempts to improve productivity. On the other side of the capitol, Senator Strom Thurmond (R-S.C.), chairman of the Senate Judiciary Committee, will hold hearings on recommendations for the refocus of U.S. antitrust laws. Conglomerate mergers and how they should be treated in antitrust law are certain to receive prominent attention. Publicity over the attempts of large firms to acquire CONOCO, as this goes to press, has spurred renewed interest in legislation to deal with the merger of major corporations.

# Notes to Text

[1] Lawrence Sullivan, *Antitrust* (St. Paul, Minn.: West Publishing Co., 1977), pp. 577–81. See also William Letwin, *Law and Economic Policy in America* (New York: Random House, 1965), pp. 8–9; United States v. E. C. Knight Co., 156 U.S. 1 (1895).

[2] Jesse Markham, "Survey of the Evidence and Findings on Mergers" (Paper prepared for the Conference on Business Concentration and Price Policy, Princeton, N.J., June 17–19, 1955), pp. 7–16. Multifirm consolidations were common: one estimate suggests that 75 percent of the mergers during the 1895–1904 period involved at least five firms. Ralph Nelson, *Merger Movements in American History, 1895–1956* (Princeton, N.J.: Princeton University Press, 1959), pp. 28–29. The height of the wave was reached in 1901, with the combination of an estimated 785 plants to form the United States Steel Corporation. F. M. Scherer, *Industrial Market Structure and Economic Performance,* 2d ed. (Chicago: Rand McNally, 1980), p. 121.

[3] Sullivan, *Antitrust,* p. 581; Markham, "Survey of the Evidence and Findings on Mergers," pp. 11–12, commenting on John Moody, *The Truth about Trusts* (New York (?): Moody Publishing Company, 1904; reprint ed., Westport, Conn.: Greenwood Press, 1970). Among the industries affected were copper, lead, railroad cars, explosives, chemicals, tin cans, tobacco products, electrical equipment, rubber products, paper, farm machinery, brickmaking, leather, shoe machinery, sugar, photographic equipment, and business machines. Scherer, *Industrial Market Structure,* p. 121.

[4] 193 U.S. 197 (1904).

[5] Sullivan, *Antitrust*, p. 583.

[6] The Standard Oil Co. of New Jersey v. United States, 221 U.S. 1 (1911); United States v. American Tobacco Co., 221 U.S. 106 (1911).

[7] Sullivan, *Antitrust,* p. 588. See also David Martin, *Mergers and the Clayton Act* (Berkeley, Calif.: University of California Press, 1959), pp. 23–29.

[8] The Clayton Act of October 15, 1914, 15 U.S.C. 12–27; the Federal Trade Commission Act of September 26, 1914, 15 U.S.C. 41–51.

[9] This new merger wave began in the year when the Supreme Court decided United States v. United States Steel Corp., 251 U.S. 417 (1920), a ruling characterized as "the rule of reason case which best exemplifies a judicial washing of hands of the structural problem." Sullivan, *Antitrust,* p. 587; see Scherer, *Industrial Market Structure,* p. 122, for a full discussion of the differences between the first and second merger waves.

[10] The immediate impetus for the Celler-Kefauver Act, 64 Stat. 1125, 15 U.S.C. 18, was provided by the Supreme Court's ruling in United States v. Columbia Steel Co., 334 U.S. 495 (1948), the leading merger case of the 1940s. In *Columbia Steel,* the Court refused to enjoin under the Sherman Act the asset acquisition of Consolidated Steel (a large West Coast steel fabricator) by a subsidiary of the United States Steel Co.

The Antitrust Procedural Improvements Act of 1980, Public Law 96–349, amended the Clayton Act to make it applicable to "persons" rather than corporations. Thus, for the first time the act covers acquisitions involving partnerships, unincorporated associations, and other noncorporate entities. In addition, the 1980 act overruled United States v. American Building Maintenance Industries, 422 U.S. 271 (1975), holding that jurisdiction to challenge mergers under the statute obtains only if the acquiring and acquired corporations are directly engaged in the production, distribution, or acquisition of goods or services in interstate commerce. As amended, the act now employs the less stringent jurisdictional standard "affecting commerce" found in the Sherman Act and in the Federal Trade Commission Act, 15 U.S.C. 45. See Joseph P. Griffin, "Reach of Merger Statute Expanded by New Legislation," *Federal Bar News,* vol. 28 (January 1981), p. 233.

[11] 370 U.S. 294 (1962).

[12] Federal Trade Commission, Bureau of Economics, *Statistical Report on Mergers and Acquisitions,* various years. In 1977, conglomerate mergers accounted for 70 percent of mergers measured by number, and 78 percent measured by assets. The data reflect only mergers in which the acquired firm had assets of $10 million or more. See also George J. Benston, *Conglomerate Mergers: Causes, Consequences, and Remedies* (Washington, D.C.: American Enterprise Institute, 1980), pp. 5–7, and the accompanying graph, derived from testimony of F.M. Scherer, former director of the Bureau of Economics at the Federal Trade Commission, which charts the volume of mergers involving manufacturing and mining firm acquisitions from 1895 to 1978 in constant dollars. Benston attributes the current volume of mergers to (1) accounting procedures that mislead investors; (2) legislation that restricts horizontal and vertical mergers, and threats of additional antimerger legislation that encourage conglomerate mergers in particular; (3) growth and changes in enterprises that bring them to a stage of development at which mergers are rational; (4) economic disturbances that change relative perceptions about the value of companies, which leads to an increase in trading; and (5) the present economic and tax climate that makes acquisitions attractive.

[13] Private figures compiled by W. T. Grimm and Co., cited in U.S. Congress, Senate, Subcommittee on Antitrust, Monopoly, and Business Rights of the Committee on the Judiciary, *Hearings on Mergers and Economic Concentration,* 96th Congress, 1st session, 1979 (hereafter *1979 S. 600 Hearings*), vol. 1, pp. 62, 71–72, statement of John H. Shenefield, then assistant attorney general, Antitrust Division, Department of Justice. The value of assets acquired in large mergers during the peak year 1968 was $12.6 billion.

[14] For a discussion of the effect of industry concentration on prices and the behavior of firms in such markets, see, for example, Joe S. Bain, *Industrial Organization,* 2nd ed. (New York: John Wiley and Sons, 1968), pp. 114, 182–83, 189, 211, 252, 255, 270–74; Harold Demsetz, *The Market Concentration Doctrine* (Washington,

D.C.: American Enterprise Institute–Hoover Institution on War, Revolution and Peace, 1973); Yale Brozen, *The Concentration-Collusion Doctrine,* Reprint No. 93 (Washington, D.C.: American Enterprise Institute, 1978); Joseph F. Brodley, "Oligopoly Power under the Sherman and Clayton Acts: From Economic Theory to Legal Policy," *Stanford Law Review,* vol. 19 (January 1967), pp. 285, 289; Thomas W. Dunfee and Louis W. Stern, "Potential Competition Theory as an Antimerger Tool under Section 7 of the Clayton Act," *Northwestern University Law Review,* vol. 69 (January-February 1975), pp. 821–22, note 8.

[15] American Bar Association, *ABA Antitrust Developments* (1975), p. 79. Conglomerate mergers may, of course, produce significant horizontal or vertical effects and may therefore be challenged under conventional antitrust standards. Determining the extent of horizontal or vertical overlap between the merged firms, however, often raises problems of characterization. For example, the acquisition of the New York Yankees by the Columbia Broadcasting System (CBS), ultimately treated as a conglomerate merger (since baseball and television may be viewed as discrete markets), might alternatively have been classified as horizontal (by viewing the firms as rivals in the entertainment market) or vertical (since the Yankees supply programs to television). Robert H. Bork, *The Antitrust Paradox: A Policy at War with Itself* (New York: Basic Books, 1978), p. 246. To the extent that horizontal or vertical overlap is found, it may bring the entire merger, including parts with no anticompetitive effect, within the prohibition of the statutes. In that event, however, antitrust exposure can frequently be avoided by divestiture of the offending entities. U.S. Congress, Senate, Subcommittee on Antitrust and Monopoly of the Judiciary Committee, *Hearings on Mergers and Economic Concentration,* 95th Congress, 2d session, 1978 (hereafter *1978 Merger Hearings*), p. 205, statement of John H. Shenefield.

[16] United States v. Marine Bancorporation, 418 U.S. 602, 624–625, 630 (1974). See also Norman Yoerg, Jr., "Foreign Entry and Potential Competition Doctrine under Section 7 of the Clayton Act," *Antitrust Law Journal,* vol. 46 (Winter 1978), p. 973; Luke E. Sims, "The Potential Competition Doctrine after Marine Bancorporation," *Georgetown Law Journal,* vol. 63 (March 1975), pp. 969, 973.

[17] Edmund H. Mantell, "Conglomerate Mergers, Allocative Efficiency, and Section 7 of the Clayton Act," *Texas Law Review,* vol. 56 (January 1978), pp. 207, 213. Mantell criticizes potential competition theory.

[18] Joseph P. Bauer, "Challenging Conglomerate Mergers under Section 7 of the Clayton Act," *Boston University Law Review,* vol. 58 (March 1978), pp. 199, 204, 219; Sims, "The Potential Competition Doctrine after Marine Bancorporation," pp. 971–73.

[19] "United States v. Falstaff Brewing Corporation: Potential Competition Reexamined," *Michigan Law Review,* vol. 72 (March 1974), pp. 837, 852; "Potential Competition: Analysis of an Antitrust Case," *Missouri Law Review,* vol. 44 (Summer 1979), pp. 458, 477, 479.

[20] "Conglomerate Mergers: A Company will be Presumed a 'Toehold' Firm," *Harvard Law Review,* vol. 89 (February 1976), pp. 802, 804–5; G. E. Hale and Rosemary D. Hale, "Potential Competition under Section 7: The Supreme Court's Crystal Ball," *Supreme Court Review,* vol. 1964, pp. 171, 181–83. See also United

States v. Marine Bancorporation, 418 U.S. 602, 633, 638–39 (1974); Richard A. Posner, "Conglomerate Mergers and Antitrust Policy," *St. John's Law Review,* vol. 44 (Spring 1970, special edition), p. 529; Robert H. Swennes II, "Three Theories of Potential Competition under Section 7 of the Clayton Act," *Tulane Law Review,* vol. 49 (November 1974), pp. 139, 148; Joseph P. Brodley, "Potential Competition Mergers," *Yale Law Journal,* vol. 87 (November 1977), pp. 1, 65.

[21] Mantell, "Conglomerate Mergers," p. 215. One commentator argues that entry by acquisition of a major firm may be procompetitive since, if the market is already noncompetitive, there is little to lose by such an acquisition and it may in fact break down existing patterns of tacitly collusive behavior. "United States v. Falstaff Brewing Corporation: Potential Competition Reexamined," p. 866.

[22] United States v. Falstaff Brewing Corporation, 410 U.S. 526, 537 (1973); United States v. Marine Bancorporation, 418 U.S. 602, 625, and note 38 (1974). The government's challenge to acquisitions and mergers, based on the actual potential competition theory, has been rejected in a series of cases cited in Robert K. Hood, "Potential Competition," *Antitrust Bulletin,* vol. 21 (Fall 1976), pp. 485, 501, note 65. The FTC relied on the actual potential competition theory in its 1980 order to break up a joint venture. See In the Matter of Brunswick Corp., FTC Docket 9028, August 14, 1980. That order is now under review in the U.S. Court of Appeals for the Eighth Circuit.

[23] 386 U.S. 568, 578–79 (1967). Raising factual and psychological barriers to entry is cited in General Foods Corp. v. FTC, 386 F. 2d 936, 945 (3rd Cir. 1967), certiorari denied, 391 U.S. 919 (1968).

[24] General Foods Corp. v. FTC, 386 F. 2d 936, 946 (3d Cir. 1967), certiorari denied, 391 U.S. 919 (1968); see also United States v. Wilson Sporting Goods Co., 288 F. Supp. 543 (N.D. Ill. 1968).

[25] The Supreme Court also supported its conclusion about the anticompetitive effect of the acquisition in the *Clorox* case by reliance on the potential competition doctrine. Critics include Robert H. Bork, former solicitor general of the United States, who contends that neither the FTC nor the Court explained what entry barriers were present in the *Clorox* case other than superior efficiency. While the opinion can be viewed as bottomed on the protection of small businesses from competition by more efficient rivals, the Court can only provide protection, according to Bork, when cost advantages are achieved through merger, but not when such advantages accrue through internal growth. The Court's reliance on dissuasion of smaller competitors from aggressive competition is criticized on the ground that these firms will in fact be forced to cut costs, to improve their product, and to lower prices to continue in the race, so there should be no lessening of competition. Bork, *The Antitrust Paradox,* pp. 253–57.

[26] 380 U.S. 592 (1965). The concurring opinion of Justice Stewart noted that the defendant could not readily strong-arm major food processors, but a second class of food processors, composed of smaller firms that sold their products to the defendant in bulk and depended on it to persuade supermarkets to try them on their counters, were susceptible to the subtle pressures of reciprocity (p. 607). See also Brodley, "Oligopoly Power under the Sherman and Clayton Acts," pp. 285, 327–28, 361; James M. Ferguson, "Tying Arrangements and Reciprocity: An

Economic Analysis," *Law and Contemporary Problems,* vol. 30 (1965), p. 552; James H. Lurie and Paul Halpern, "Conglomerates: The Rhetoric and the Evidence," *Journal of Law and Economics,* vol. 13 (April 1970), pp. 149, 151–53.

[27] See Bork, *The Antitrust Paradox,* pp. 257–59, for criticism of the reciprocity theory.

[28] *1979 S. 600 Hearings,* vol. 2, p. 39, statement of Donald I. Baker, former assistant attorney general, Antitrust Division, Department of Justice.

[29] See, for example, Corwin Edwards, "The Conglomerate Enterprise" (Paper prepared for the Conference on Business Concentration and Price Policy), pp. 16–20.

[30] Speech by Daniel C. Schwartz, deputy director, Bureau of Competition, FTC, before the Committee on Trade Regulation, Association of the Bar of the City of New York, November 27, 1978, p. 8.

[31] United States v. Northwest Industries, Inc., 301 F. Supp. 1066, 1096 (N.D. Ill. 1969): refusal to read Section 7 as reaching trend toward economic concentration without any specific showing of substantial lessening of competition in a market. United States v. International Telephone & Telegraph Corp., 306 F. Supp. 766, 796 (D. Conn. 1969): merger increasing economic concentration, without more, deemed insufficient to justify halting merger under Section 7.

[32] For background leading to the enactment of the various antimerger statutes and references to some earlier Court decisions, see such works as Clair Wilcox, "Substantive Provisions of the Antitrust Laws," in Edwin Mansfield, ed., *Monopoly Power and Economic Performance,* 3rd ed. (New York: W. W. Norton, 1965), pp. 135–39 (the third edition is cited hereafter except as noted); Richard A. Posner, *Antitrust Law* (Chicago: University of Chicago Press, 1976), pp. 23–31; Bork, *The Antitrust Paradox,* pp. 15–19.

[33] 370 U.S. 294 (1962). The merger involved Brown Shoe Company, the third largest seller and fourth largest manufacturer of shoes in the United States with 4 percent of the nation's footwear production and G. R. Kinney Company, Inc., which manufactured less than 0.5 percent and retailed less than 2 percent of the nation's shoes.

[34] 370 U.S. 294, 315–16, 333. The Court's statement, however, that the legislative history "illuminates congressional concern with the protection of *competition,* not *competitors*" suggests a concern with competition as contemplated in economic theory rather than the preservation of small entities (see p. 320). Concern for competition and not competitors is reiterated in Brunswick Corp. v. Pueblo Bowl-O-Mat, Inc., 429 U.S. 477, 488 (1977).

[35] 370 U.S. 294, 315–16, 320, 321 note 36. The *Brown Shoe* opinion is criticized in such studies as Bork, *The Antitrust Paradox,* pp. 60, 65, 87–88, 198–216, 225–31, 247; Posner, *Antitrust Law,* pp. 100–105, 107 note 29.

[36] 374 U.S. 321 (1963). The Court admitted that neither the statute nor its legislative history suggests that any particular percentage of market share is critical (pp. 362, 365). In United States v. El Paso Natural Gas Company, 376 U.S. 651 (1964), the

Court relied on potential competition theory to find that the acquisition of a firm in an oligopolistic market was anticompetitive.

[37] 377 U.S. 271 (1964). After the decision of the *Philadelphia National Bank* case and before the decision to the *Aluminum Company* case, the Court applied potential competition doctrine to find that the acquisition involved in United States v. El Paso Natural Gas Company, 376 U.S. 651 (1964), essentially a horizontal merger, might substantially lessen competition.

[38] 378 U.S. 158. The criteria cited are:

> The number and power of the competitors in the relevant market; the background of their growth; the power of the joint venturers; the relationship of their lines of commerce; the competition existing between them and the power of each in dealing with the competitors of the other; the setting in which the joint venture was created; the reasons and necessities for its existence; the joint venture's line of commerce and the relationship thereof to that of its parents; the adaptability of its line of commerce to noncompetitive practices; the potential power of the joint venture in the relevant market; an appraisal of what the competition in the relevant market would have been if one of the joint venturers had entered it alone instead of through Penn-Olin [the joint venture]; the effect, in the event of this occurrence, of the other joint venturer's potential competition; and such other factors as might indicate potential risk to competition in the relevant market (p. 177).

[39] Hood, "Potential Competition," pp. 493–94.

[40] 378 U.S. 441 (1964). The Court treated cans and glass jars but not plastic containers as competing in the relevant market and ruled that the acquisition of Hazel-Atlas Glass Company by Continental Can, a horizontal merger under this view of the market, was anticompetitive.

[41] 384 U.S. 270 (1966).The Court's decision is criticized in Bork, *The Antitrust Paradox,* pp. 205, 210, 217–18; and Posner, *Antitrust Law,* pp. 105–9.

[42] 384 U.S. 546, 550–51 (1966).

[43] 386 U.S. 568 (1967).

[44] 386 U.S. 568, 583. Justice Douglas's opinion rejected the notion that possible economies from the acquisition (efficiency) could be used as a defense (p. 580). For criticism of the majority opinion, see Hood, "Potential Competition," p. 497; Bork, *The Antitrust Paradox,* pp. 204, 210, 252–56, 260; Posner, *Antitrust Law,* p. 118. In a 1972 decision authored by Justice Douglas, Ford Motor Co. v. United States, 405 U.S. 562, the Court followed the approach taken in *Proctor & Gamble* and invalidated a vertical merger involving a major auto manufacturer and a spark-plug manufacturer with 15 percent of the domestic market.

[45] Bauer, "Challenging Conglomerate Mergers under Section 7 of the Clayton Act," p. 199; "Antitrust: Merger Law Weakened by Lack in Controlling Conglomerates," *Bureau of National Affairs Daily Report for Executives* (hereafter *BNA DER*),

November 2, 1979. Milton D. Stewart, chief counsel for advocacy at the Small Business Administration, stated that, "between 1964 and 1977, the Department of Justice won 11 conglomerate cases, and lost 22, with 12 of these losses occurring since 1974." House Report 96–1447, p. 20.

[46] 415 U.S. 486 (1974).A splintering of the justices' views on antimerger issues occurred in the earlier case of United States v. Falstaff Brewing Corp., 440 U.S. 526 (1973). Justice Byron R. White wrote an opinion for himself and two other justices remanding the case for consideration of the potential competition doctrine. Two justices wrote separate opinions, two dissented, and two did not participate in the case. See Hood, "Potential Competition," pp. 498–502. The *Falstaff* opinion is criticized in Posner, *Antitrust Law,* pp. 120–22, 125.

[47] 418 U.S. 602 (1974). One scholar has criticized this decision of the Court as an abandonment of the simplified presumptive standard employed in the *Philadelphia Bank* case in favor of a highly complicated standard that will force parties to antimerger litigation to devote enormous litigation resources to the prosecution and defense of such cases. Brodley, "Potential Competition Mergers," pp. 5–6.

[48] 433 U.S. 36 (1977). The Court noted that such restrictions promote interbrand competition even though they reduce intrabrand competition. "Per se rules of illegality are appropriate only when they relate to conduct that is manifestly anticompetitive" (pp. 49–51). Bork argues that the decision recognizes that vertical restraints make distribution more efficient, that business efficiency is used to help justify such practices under antitrust law, and that concern for efficiencies implies that a major end of antitrust law is consumer welfare. Robert H. Bork, "Vertical Restraints, Schwinn Overruled," *The Supreme Court Review,* vol. 1977, pp. 171, 180, 186. Similar emphasis on the *economic* consequences of the action challenged in a Sherman Act antitrust suit is evident in National Society of Professional Engineers v. United States, 435 U.S. 679 (1978), upholding an injunction against enforcement of a professional society's canon of ethics that prohibited association members from submitting competitive bids for engineering services. The meaning of the "rule of reason" applied in antitrust cases is also discussed (pp. 687–92).

[49] "Mobil's CONOCO Bid Sparks Moves by Justice Agency and Legislators," *Wall Street Journal*, July 20, 1981, p. 30. Although it is difficult to estimate the number of firms that would be affected by S. 600, the staff director for the Senate Judiciary Committee during the 96th Congress estimated that all provisions of the bill would affect about 900 corporations. The $2 billion cutoff would affect the nation's 128 top industries according to the *Fortune* 500 list. J. J. Pickle, "Conglomerate Mergers," *Congressional Record,* vol. 125 (April 2, 1979), pp. E 1466, E 1468.

[50] See the text of the Industrial Reorganization Act in Harvey Goldschmid, H. Michael Mann, and J. Fred Weston, eds., *Industrial Concentration: The New Learning* (Boston: Little, Brown & Co., 1974), pp. 444–48. For an earlier proposal to enforce restrictions on "unreasonable market power," see Carl Kaysen and Donald F. Turner, *Antitrust Policy* (Cambridge, Mass.: Harvard University Press, 1965), pp. 266–72.

[51] The Concentrated Industries Act is reprinted with comments in Goldschmid, Mann, and Weston, *Industrial Concentration: The New Learning,* pp. 449–56.

[52] Joe Sims, "Report of the President's Commission on Antitrust," *Regulation: AEI Journal on Government and Society,* vol. 3 (March–April 1979), pp. 25, 31–32.

[53] See *1979 S. 600 Hearings,* vol. 1, p. 232, statement of Alfred F. Dougherty, Jr., then director, Bureau of Competition, Federal Trade Commission; and see "Antitrust: FTC Official Sets Out 'No-Fault' Monopolization Theory," *BNA DER,* October 17, 1978, p. A–16. The FTC proposal would affect approximately 250 firms. Pickle, "Conglomerate Mergers," p. E 1468.

[54] Speech by Ky P. Ewing, Jr., then deputy assistant attorney general for the Antitrust Division, before the Antitrust and Trade Regulation Committee of the Westchester-Fairfield Corporation Counsel Association, Stamford, Conn., November 1, 1979, p. 32. See also *1979 S. 600 Hearings,* vol. 1, pp. 69–70, statement of Shenefield. The Justice Department proposal would affect about 242 firms. Pickle, "Conglomerate Mergers," p. E 1468.

[55] March 9, 1979, letter from then FTC Commissioner Elizabeth Hanford Dole to Senator Edward M. Kennedy, then chairman of the Senate Judiciary Committee, *Congressional Record,* vol. 126 (March 26, 1979), p. S 3363.

[56] See documents filed in the FTC Public Reference Room, including suggested draft rules, the FTC statement released October 7, 1980, and the additional statement of Commissioner Robert Pitofsky. The May 28, 1980, notice to staff concerning the effect of the FTC Improvements Act of 1980 notes at page 13 that the act removed the commission's authority to promulgate a trade regulation rule under Section 18 of the FTC Act, but it maintains that this did not affect the FTC's authority to engage in antitrust rulemaking. For a discussion of the use of a trade regulation rule to control conglomerate mergers and of a proposed rule, see Peter C. Carstensen and Nina H. Questal, "The Use of Section 5 of the FTC Act to Attack Large Conglomerate Mergers," *Cornell Law Review,* vol. 63 (June 1978), pp. 841, 866, 872–73.

[57] See, for example, the earlier proposal of Sumner H. Slichter that voluntary splits be encouraged by relieving stockholders from liability for capital gains taxes on the appreciation of their holdings from the time they purchased their stock to the date of the split. Sumner H. Slichter, "In Defense of Bigness in Business," in Mansfield, *Monopoly Power and Economic Performance,* p. 18.

[58] See the discussion in Yale Brozen, *The Antitrust Task Force Deconcentration Recommendation,* Reprint No. 14 (Washington, D.C.: American Enterprise Institute, April 1973), p. 284 and note 13.

[59] *1979 S. 600 Hearings,* vol. 2, p. 137, statement of F. M. Scherer, professor of economics, Northwestern University, *1978 Merger Hearings,* p. 160, statement of Michael Pertschuk, former chairman, now commissioner, FTC.

[60] *1979 S. 600 Hearings,* vol. 2, p. 137, statement of Scherer. Scherer explains in his testimony that these figures reflect both upward and downward biases. A 1965 study by John McGowan found that mergers accounted for two-thirds of the increase in the concentration ratio for *Fortune* 500 firms between 1950 and 1960, and for almost three-fourths of the increase in the concentration ratio for the largest

100 firms. "Conglomerate Mergers: A Study of Competition, Power, and Philosophy," *BNA DER,* July 18, 1980, p. C–4.

[61] Joe S. Bain, "Relation of Profit-Rate to Industry Concentration: American Manufacturing, 1936–1940," *Quarterly Journal of Economics,* vol. 65 (August 1951), p. 293.

[62] See an enumeration of these studies in Leonard W. Weiss, "The Concentration-Profits Relationship and Antitrust," in Goldschmid, Mann, and Weston, *Industrial Concentration: The New Learning,* pp. 184, 201–31. A recent study by John E. Kwoka, Jr., of FTC, employing a sample of 314 industries suggests that the traditional rule-of-thumb—the four-firm concentration ratio—is flawed. Kwoka found that 91 industries had a two-firm concentration ratio in excess of 35 percent. Kwoka found that when two firms control 35 percent of a market, the price-cost margins rise significantly but, if a third firm has 15 percent or more of the market, the third firm tends to increase competition. Kwoka acknowledges that the structure of the market explains only about one-fifth of the variance in industry price-cost margins. "Antitrust: FTC Economist Casts Doubt on Four-Firm Concentration Ratios," *BNA DER,* October 10, 1978, p. A–1.

[63] Mark J. Green, *The Closed Enterprise System* (New York: Grossman Publishers, 1972), p. 14.

[64] "Should There Be a Ban on Big Company Mergers?" *American Legion,* vol. 108 (October 1979), p. 8, statement of Senator Orrin Hatch (R-Utah).

[65] *1979 S. 600 Hearings,* vol. 1, p. 430, statement of Jesse W. Markham, professor of business administration, Harvard University; Paul W. McCracken and Thomas Gale Moore, *Competition and Market Concentration in the American Economy,* Reprint No. 25 (Washington, D.C.: American Enterprise Institute, 1974), pp. 6–7.

[66] *1979 S. 600 Hearings,* vol. 1, pp. 603–4, statement of David Schwartzman, New School for Social Research; ibid., p. 461, statement of Michael Gort, professor of economics, State University of New York at Buffalo; ibid., vol. 2, pp. 342–43, statement of L. Earle Birdzell, consultant to the National Chamber Foundation, an affiliate of the Chamber of Commerce of the United States.

[67] "Conglomerate Mergers: A Study of Competition, Power, and Philosophy," p. C–5.

[68] Benston, *Conglomerate Mergers: Causes, Consequences, and Remedies,* pp. 57–60. Betty Bock, director of antitrust research for the Conference Board and adjunct professor of law at New York University, detailed the difficulties in deriving the denominators and numerators of aggregate concentration ratios in *1979 S. 600 Hearings,* vol. 1, pp. 507–11. Others note that alternative measures of aggregate concentration will lead to substantial fluctuations in the numbers; ibid., pp. 541–43, statement of J. Fred Weston, professor, Graduate School of Business, University of California at Los Angeles. Some studies emphasize concentration figures from manufacturing industries. These industries, however, account for only about one-fourth of the output and employment in the economy. Milton Friedman, "Monopoly and Social Responsibility of Business and Labor," in Mansfield, *Mo-*

*nopoly Power and Economic Performance,* p. 60. Friedman notes that firms that have grown larger as the economy has grown are perceived as capturing a larger fraction of the market when in fact the market may have grown faster than the market share of these companies. In other words, economic growth can aid in the deconcentration of industry. Weston believes that industrial concentration principally involves industries where firms come in large sizes, such as the oil industry, and that the total number of businesses continues to rise, increasing approximately 25 percent between 1960 and 1975, from 11 million to 14 million firms. Bock maintains that, if we put to one side the 61 corporations in petroleum, coal, and chemicals from the largest 200 firms in assets in 1977, the remaining 139 corporations declined in assets in the period from 1972 to 1979. "Conglomerate Mergers: A Study of Competition, Power, and Philosophy," p. C–4.

[69] *1979 S. 600 Hearings,* vol. 2, p. 315, statement of Birdzell. Scholars point to the conclusions of economist Leonard Weiss of the University of Wisconsin at Madison that, if we could determine a critical concentration ratio or ratios (perhaps by producer and consumer goods separately), the antitrust authorities could safely permit mergers that increase concentration short of the critical level. Within that range, increased concentration would gain economies of scale without undesirable price effects. Leonard W. Weiss, "The Structure Conduct-Performance Paradigm and Antitrust," *University of Pennsylvania Law Review,* vol. 127 (April 1979), pp. 1104, 1118–19.

[70] *1979 S. 600 Hearings,* vol. 1, pp. 583–84, statement of Schwartzman; McCracken and Moore, *Competition and Market Concentration,* pp. 4–5; Bain, *Industrial Organization,* p. 92.

[71] Joseph A. Schumpeter, *Capitalism, Socialism, and Democracy,* 3rd ed. (New York: Harper and Row, 1950), pp. 82–83.

[72] John Kenneth Galbraith, *The New Industrial State* (Boston: Houghton Mifflin Co., 1967), pp. 74–77; John Kenneth Galbraith, *American Capitalism* (Boston: Houghton Mifflin Co., 1952), p. 91; John Kenneth Galbraith, "The Economics of Technical Development," in Mansfield, *Monopoly Power and Economic Performance,* p. 37.

[73] Willard T. Carleton, Robert S. Harris, and John F. Stewart, *An Empirical Study of Merger Motives* (Washington, D.C.: Federal Trade Commission, December 1980), p. 96, note 1.

[74] Bain, *Industrial Organization,* pp. 182–83; Richard R. Nelson and Sidney G. Winter, "Forces Generating and Limiting Concentration under Schumpeterian Competition," *The Bell Journal of Economics,* vol. 9 (August 1978), pp. 524, 541.

[75] Brozen, *The Antitrust Task Force Deconcentration Recommendation;* Brozen, *The Concentration-Collusion Doctrine;* Harold Demsetz, "Two Systems of Belief about Monopoly," in Goldschmid, Mann, and Weston, *Industrial Concentration: The New Learning,* pp. 164, 168–78; Demsetz, *The Market Concentration Doctrine.* Demsetz claims that empirical data show that only one or two firms are making large profits in concentrated industries and that, if collusion were in fact involved, all or most of the firms in an industry would make large profits. "Antitrust: Econ-

omists Preach Gospel of Harm to Consumers," *BNA DER,* August 30, 1978, pp. C–1, C–2.

[76] McCracken and Moore, *Competition and Market Concentration,* pp. 5, 7–9; Benston, *Conglomerate Mergers: Causes, Consequences, and Remedies,* p. 51; Slichter, "In Defense of Bigness in Business," pp. 15–17; "Conglomerate Mergers: A Study of Competition, Power, and Philosophy," p. C–9, citing Robert H. Bork.

[77] Orrin Hatch, "Antitrust Divestiture and Ancillary Restraints in the Petroleum Industry," *Congressional Record,* vol. 126 (September 11, 1980), pp. S 12411, 12419; "A New Worst in Antitrust," in Mansfield, *Monopoly Power and Economic Performance,* p. 188; Slichter, "In Defense of Bigness in Business," p. 16. Galbraith contends that current antimerger enforcement efforts protect the market power of very large firms by diligent harassment of firms with less market power that seek to merge. John Kenneth Galbraith, "The New Industrial State," in Mansfield, *Monopoly Power and Economic Performance,* pp. 198, 200; Irving S. Shapiro, "The Antitrust Syndrome: Is Bigness Bad?" *Vital Speeches of the Day,* vol. 45 (July 1, 1979), pp. 561–62.

[78] Dale Bumpers, "The Concentration of Economic Power," *Congressional Record,* vol. 126 (April 18, 1980), p. S 3915; Walter Adams, "The Antitrust Alternative," in Ralph Nader and Mark J. Green, eds., *Corporate Power in America* (New York: Grossman Publishers, 1973), pp. 130, 134–38; Weiss, "The Concentration-Profits Relationship and Antitrust," pp. 184, 232.

[79] Donald F. Turner, "The Antitrust Chief Replies," in Mansfield, *Monopoly Power and Economic Performance,* pp. 190, 192–93.

[80] Weiss, "The Concentration-Profits Relationship and Antitrust," pp. 231–32.

[81] See, for example, Abba Lerner, "Monopoly Power: Causes of Inflation at Less Than Full Employment," in Mansfield, *Monopoly Power and Economic Performance,* pp. 201–2, on price controls; Kenneth W. Dam, "The 'Big Is Bad' Bill," *Wall Street Journal,* May 22, 1979, citing nationalization of ailing firms in other countries.

[82] See, for example, George J. Stigler, *The Theory of Price,* 3rd ed. (New York: Macmillan, 1966), p. 236. The meat-packing industry maxim is quoted in Hale and Hale, "Potential Competition under Section 7: The Supreme Court's Crystal Ball," p. 172.

[83] Richard A. Posner, "The Chicago School of Antitrust Analysis," *University of Pennsylvania Law Review,* vol. 127 (April 1979), pp. 925, 929–32, 945–47. Posner claims that the cost of a major new plant will be amortized by the new entrant over time and that the existing firms face the same annual costs if they plan to replace their plants. The cost of capital may be somewhat higher for a new entrant if there is uncertainty about its likely success in the market but, again, the risk premium is but a fraction of capital costs and a much smaller fraction of overall costs.

[84] Demsetz, "Two Systems of Belief about Monopoly," pp. 164, 181; and see Walter Adams, "Corporate Power and Economic Apologetics: A Public Policy Perspec-

tive," in Goldschmid, Mann, and Weston, *Industrial Concentration: The New Learning,* pp. 360, 374–95.

[85] Edwards, "The Conglomerate Enterprise," pp. 16–20; Adams, "Corporate Power and Economic Apologetics," p. 368, quoting from Corwin D. Edwards, "Conglomerate Business as a Source of Power," in National Bureau of Economic Research, ed., *Business Concentration and Price Policy* (Princeton, N.J.: Princeton University Press, 1955), p. 335.

[86] *1978 Merger Hearings,* p. 181, statement of Walter Adams, professor of economics, Michigan State University.

[87] See John M. Blair, "The Conglomerate Merger in Economics and Law," *Georgetown Law Journal,* vol. 46 (1958), p. 672; Corwin Edwards, "The Large Conglomerate Firm: A Critical Appraisal," in Mansfield, *Monopoly Power and Economic Performance,* pp. 111–12; Richard Craswell, "Antitrust Policy Issues Raised by Some Business Strategy Models," in *Papers on Business Strategy and Antitrust* (Washington, D.C.: Federal Trade Commission, September 1980), p. 12.

[88] *1978 Merger Hearings,* pp. 93–94, statement of Willard F. Mueller, professor of economics, University of Wisconsin.

[89] Craswell, "Antitrust Policy Issues Raised by Some Business Strategy Models," p. 30. Scholars disagree about whether pricing below marginal costs, below fully distributed costs, below average costs, or below some other benchmark should be considered predatory for antitrust enforcement purposes. Professors Areeda and Turner, recognizing the difficulty of measuring marginal costs, recommended that only prices set below average variable costs (that is, costs exclusive of fixed costs) should be considered predatory. Phillip Areeda and Donald Turner, "Predatory Pricing and Related Practices under Section 2 of the Sherman Act," *Harvard Law Review,* vol. 88 (February 1975), p. 697. A number of courts have adopted this test or a slight variation of it, in part because it can be administered with less difficulty than some other tests. That rule is much criticized and various scholars have proposed alternatives. For a discussion of this problem see Posner, "The Chicago School of Antitrust Analysis," pp. 939–44; Paul L. Joskow and Alvin K. Klevorick, "A Framework for Analyzing Predatory Pricing Policy," *Yale Law Journal,* vol. 89 (December 1979), p. 213; Sims, "Report of the President's Commission on Antitrust," p. 30; and the series of articles and cases cited in John J. Siegfried, ed., *The Economics of Firm Size, Market Structure, and Social Performance* (Washington, D.C.: Federal Trade Commission, July 1980), pp. 12–13, 84–85.

[90] Bork, *The Antitrust Paradox,* p. 146 and p. 154, citing Areeda and Turner. Bork refers to earlier studies of instances in which predation is said to have occurred and notes the conclusions of scholars that predation did not in fact exist in a high percentage of the court cases examined. Ibid., pp. 144, 152–55, citing John McGee, "Predatory Price Cutting: The Standard Oil (N.J.) Case," *Journal of Law and Economics,* vol. 1 (1958), p. 137; M. A. Adelman, *A & P: A Study in Price-Cost Behavior and Public Policy* (Cambridge, Mass.: Harvard University Press, 1966); Kenneth G. Elzinga, "Predatory Pricing: The Case of the Gunpowder Trust," *Journal of Law and Economics,* vol. 13 (April 1970), p. 223; Ronald H. Koller II,

"The Myth of Predatory Pricing: An Empirical Study," *Antitrust Law and Economic Review,* vol. 4 (Summer 1971), p. 105. See also "Conglomerate Mergers: A Study of Competition, Power, and Philosophy," p. C–10, statement of Scherer, regarding the lack of likelihood that losses from price cutting can be recouped or that conglomerate size will lead to anticompetitive effects.

[91] Donald E. Turner, "Conglomerate Mergers and Section 7 of the Clayton Act," *Harvard Law Review,* vol. 78 (May 1965), pp. 1313, 1360; "Acquisition of Leading Coal Company by Potential Entrant into Coal Industry Violated Section 7 of the Clayton Act," *Harvard Law Review,* vol. 86 (February 1973), pp. 772, 783. See also Bork, *The Antitrust Paradox,* pp. 147–48. Bork quotes Stigler to the effect that capital (or credit) is the most mobile of all resources and contends that, if a potential victim of predation would find it profitable to resist predation by use of its liquid assets, a lender should find it equally profitable to lend the required capital.

[92] Bork, *The Antitrust Paradox,* pp. 148, 152–53. Du Pont, the lowest-cost producer of titanium dioxide, was charged with an attempt to monopolize the market by expanding production and keeping prices low to discourage competitors' expansion of capacity. The issue was, absent proof of illegal pricing below cost, whether du Pont had alternative courses of action it was required to take to avoid running afoul of the law. The FTC concluded that its cost advantage was the result of foresight, the taking of economic risk, and so forth, and ruled that du Pont need not license its technology to its competitors or divest itself of certain production facilities. *BNA Antitrust and Trade Regulation Reporter,* No. 931, September 20, 1979, p. A–1.

[93] Bork, *The Antitrust Paradox,* pp. 145, 154; Jesse W. Markham, "The Large Conglomerate Firm: A Different View," in Mansfield, *Monopoly Power and Economic Performance,* pp. 116–17.

[94] Posner, "The Chicago School of Antitrust Analysis," p. 927. Bork contends that a shoe retailer can be driven out quickly by predation but that reentry, when prices return to normal levels, will be equally rapid. Railroading with its specialized facilities would be difficult to enter but the potential victim of predation will be difficult to drive out precisely because railroad facilities are not useful to other industries. Bork, *The Antitrust Paradox,* pp. 153, 251.

[95] *1979 S. 600 Hearings,* vol. 1, p. 38, statement of Ralph Nader and Mark Green, consumer activists.

[96] Bork, *The Antitrust Paradox,* pp. 254–55.

[97] Dennis C. Mueller, "Conglomerates: A 'Nonindustry,' " in Walter Adams, ed., *The Structure of American Industry,* 5th ed. (New York: Macmillan, 1977), pp. 472, 475. See also *1979 S. 600 Hearings,* vol. 1, p. 65, statement of Shenefield; Edwards, "The Large Conglomerate Firm: A Critical Appraisal," in Mansfield, *Monopoly Power and Economic Performance,* pp. 110, 113–14; Phillip Areeda and Donald Turner, "Conglomerate Mergers: Extended Interdependence and Effects on Interindustry Competition as Grounds for Condemnation," *University of Pennsylvania Law Review,* vol. 127 (April 1979), pp. 1082–84; Carleton, Harris, and Stewart, *An Empirical Study of Merger Motives,* p. 9.

[98] Areeda and Turner, "Conglomerate Mergers: Extended Interdependence and Effects on Interindustry Competition," p. 1091. These scholars cite the following prerequisites for mutual forbearance from conglomeration: (1) the merged firm and at least one rival must confront each other in two markets, each of which is somewhat oligopolistic in performance but not rigidly so; (2) the merged firm and at least one other two-market firm must both be significant in both markets, and both markets must be relatively important to both firms; and (3) a firm, to be deterred from a price cut in one market, must be subject to sanctions in a second market. Turner and Areeda also note that a firm would rarely plan a conglomerate acquisition to foster extended interdependence. A firm with a strong position in one market would have no incentive to acquire a vulnerable firm in a second market if the principal effect of that acquisition would be to reduce its ability to make profit-maximizing moves in the first market. Nor is there any reason for a firm vulnerable in one market to acquire a strong firm in a second market if vulnerability in the first market reduced its perceived ability to exploit the strong position in the second market. Ibid., pp. 1084–89.

[99] Edwards, "The Large Conglomerate Firm: A Critical Appraisal," p. 113.

[100] Mueller, "Conglomerates," pp. 465, 471.

[101] See FTC v. Consolidated Food Corp., 380 U.S. 592 (1965).

[102] Bork, *The Antitrust Paradox,* p. 258; Lawrence W. Keeshan, "Conglomerate Mergers and the Theory of Reciprocity," *Stanford Law Review,* vol. 22 (April 1970), pp. 812, 823.

[103] Edwards, "The Large Conglomerate Firm: A Critical Appraisal," p. 112. See also *1979 S. 600 Hearings,* vol. 1, p. 65, statement of Shenefield; FTC v. Procter & Gamble Co., 386 U.S. 568, 578 (1967); Turner, "Conglomerate Mergers and Section 7 of the Clayton Act," pp. 1313, 1351, 1358.

[104] Bork, *The Antitrust Paradox,* p. 257.

[105] *1979 S. 600 Hearings,* vol. 1, p. 39, statement of Nader and Green. See also F.M. Scherer, "Economies of Scale and Industrial Concentration," in Goldschmid, Mann, and Weston, *Industrial Concentration: The New Learning,* pp. 16, 49; Jesse W. Markham, "Concentration: A Stimulus or Retardant to Innovation?" in Goldschmid, Mann, and Weston, *Industrial Concentration: The New Learning,* p. 263, citing Scherer; Morton I. Kamien and Nancy L. Schwartz, "Market Structure and Innovation: A Survey," *Journal of Economic Literature,* vol. 13 (March 1975), pp. 1, 32 (article lists 100 references to earlier studies on the titled subject). Michael Pertschuk and Kenneth M. Davidson, "What's Wrong with Conglomerate Mergers?" *Fordham Law Review,* vol. 48 (October 1979), pp. 1, 16. A major study by the National Science Foundation for the 1953–1973 period is cited to show that small firms produced about twenty-three times as many major innovations as large firms per research and development (R & D) dollar spent, and small firms had a ratio of innovations to R & D employees four times greater than large firms. "Conglomerate Mergers: A Study of Competition, Power, and Philosophy," p. C–13.

[106] Scherer, "Economies of Scale and Industrial Concentration," pp. 48–49.

[107] Walter Adams, "Another View of the New Industrial State," in Mansfield, *Monopoly Power and Economic Performance,* pp. 130–31.

[108] *1979 S. 600 Hearings,* vol. 1, p. 65, statement of Shenefield.

[109] Edwin Mansfield, "Monopoly Power, Big Business and Technological Change," in Mansfield, *Monopoly Power and Economic Performance,* p. 53.

[110] Kamien and Schwartz, "Market Structure and Innovation: A Survey," p. 14, citing Schumpeter, Galbraith, Villard, and G. Warren Nutter; Henry H. Villard, "Competition, Oligopoly, and Research," *Journal of Political Economy,* vol. 66 (December 1958), p. 483; Edwin Mansfield, "Size of Firm, Market Structure, and Innovation," *Journal of Political Economy,* vol. 71 (December 1963), pp. 556–57; "Conglomerate Mergers: A Study of Competition, Power, and Philosophy," p. D–10; A. D. H. Kaplan, *Big Enterprise in a Competitive System* (Washington, D.C.: Brookings Institution, 1964), p. 181.

[111] Markham, "Concentration: A Stimulus or Retardant to Innovation?" p. 268; Shapiro, "The Antitrust Syndrome: Is Bigness Bad?" p. 563.

[112] See Craswell, "Antitrust Policy Issues Raised by Some Business Strategy Models," pp. 12, 16.

[113] *1979 S. 600 Hearings,* vol. 1, p. 431, statement of Markham; Richard Nelson, Merton Peck, and Edward Kalichek, "The Concentration of Research and Development in Large Firms," in Mansfield, *Monopoly Power and Economic Performance,* p. 46. The Office of Federal Procurement Policy found that firms with more than 1,000 employees spent twice as much on research and development per scientist and engineer as did firms with less than 1,000 employees. "Conglomerate Mergers: A Study of Competition, Power, and Philosophy," p. C–13. For the variation in the percentage of profits and of sales spent on R & D by eleven industries, see Senate Report 96–444, p. 39, table 11.

[114] Markham, "Concentration: A Stimulus or Retardant to Innovation?" p. 268; Nelson, Peck, and Kalichek, "The Concentration of Research and Development in Large Firms," p. 46; Galbraith, "The Economics of Technical Development," p. 39; Slichter, "In Defense of Bigness in Business," p. 17.

[115] "Conglomerate Mergers: A Study of Competition, Power, and Philosophy," p. C–14.

[116] *1978 Merger Hearings,* pp. 211–12, statement of Shenefield.

[117] *1979 S. 600 Hearings,* vol. 2, pp. 39–40, statement of Baker.

[118] *1978 Merger Hearings,* p. 259, statement of Arthur Burck, corporate merger expert; ibid., pp. 209–10, statement of Shenefield; Bumpers, "The Concentration of Economic Power," p. S 3915, citing Scherer and Harold M. Williams, chairman of the Securities and Exchange Commission; and see House Report 96–1447, pp. 25–26, citing statement of Harold M. Williams.

[119] Senate Report 96–444, p. 45.

[120] *1979 S. 600 Hearings,* vol. 2, p. 25, statement of William F. Baxter, then a

professor of law at Stanford University and currently assistant attorney general, Antitrust Division, Department of Justice.

[121] Ibid., vol. 1, p. 423, statement of Yale Brozen, professor of economics, University of Chicago.

[122] Senate Report 96–444, p. 45, statement of Shenefield; Benston, *Conglomerate Mergers: Causes, Consequences, and Remedies,* p. 24; Wayne E. Boucher, *The Process of Conglomerate Mergers* (Washington, D.C.: Federal Trade Commission, June 1980), p. 142.

[123] Turner, "Conglomerate Mergers and Section 7 of the Clayton Act," p. 1316. For the number of new business incorporations, see Benston, *Conglomerate Mergers: Causes, Consequences, and Remedies,* p. 25, table 1; and see "Conglomerate Mergers: A Study of Competition, Power, and Philosophy," pp. C–9, C–12; Jesse W. Markham, "Merger Policy under the New Section 7," *Virginia Law Review,* vol. 43 (May 1957), pp. 489, 499.

[124] J. Fred Weston, "Industrial Concentration, Mergers, and Growth: A Summary," and "Response to Reynolds' Review," in *Mergers and Economic Efficiency,* vol. 1 (Washington, D.C.: U.S. Department of Commerce, 1980), pp. 38, 43, 80, 87. Markham contends that conglomerates add to the efficiency of capital markets because they operate on the frontier of a great many industries and have better information on the marginal effect of capital on a large number of activities. *Mergers and Economic Efficiency,* p. 10.

[125] *1979 S. 600 Hearings,* vol. 2, p. 15, statement of Richard A. Posner, professor of law, University of Chicago. Brozen cites a study of all New York Stock Exchange firms acquired since 1945 to show that the earnings of stockholders of these acquired firms steadily declined and afforded below-normal rates of return in the four-year period ending four months before the acquisition of their firms. The stockholders were then made whole, and their stock rose an additional 8 percent after the acquisition and subsequently earned a normal rate of return on formerly badly managed assets. Yale Brozen, "A Comment on Weston's Industrial Concentration, Mergers, and Growth," in *Mergers and Economic Efficiency,* pp. 63, 65; see also Brozen's comments at pp. 15 and 27. Brozen also cites data on value added per employee by multi-industry firms contrasted with value added per employee in single-industry firms in 1954, 1963, and 1972, with the differences ranging from 15 percent to 30 percent. This, according to Brozen, demonstrates the increased efficiency of conglomerate enterprise. Ibid., pp. 65–68.

[126] Weston, "Industrial Concentration, Mergers, and Growth: A Summary," p. 43; Weston, "Response to Reynolds' Review," p. 86; Senate Report 96–444, p. 139; editorial, *St. Louis Globe-Democrat,* June 30, 1979; Brozen comments in *Mergers and Economic Efficiency,* p. 16. The takeover of firms having low returns leads to more efficient use of capital resources, it is claimed, and the provision of more competent management protects the interests of the vast number of small noncontrolling shareholders. Donald R. Kummen and J. Ronald Hoffmeister, "Valuation Consequences of Cash Tender Offers," *Journal of Finance,* vol. 33 (May 1978), pp. 505, 515–16. Kummen and Hoffmeister contend that in friendly takeovers both firms realize benefits.

[127] Turner, "Conglomerate Mergers and Section 7 of the Clayton Act," p. 1316; Bain, *Industrial Organization,* p. 166 and following. Benston also cites the possibility of lowering administrative costs, particularly those imposed by government regulatory agencies such as the Environmental Protection Agency (EPA) and the Occupational Safety and Health Administration (OSHA), and by the requirements of the Employee Retirement Income Security Act of 1974 (ERISA). Benston, *Conglomerate Mergers: Causes, Consequences, and Remedies,* p. 32.

[128] *1979 S. 600 Hearings,* vol. 1, p. 172, statement of Dougherty; Weston, "Industrial Concentration, Mergers, and Growth: A Summary," p. 39; Weston, "Response to Reynolds' Review," p. 81; Shelby Bryan, "Conglomerate Mergers: Proposed Guidelines," *Harvard Journal on Legislation,* vol. 11 (December 1973), pp. 31, 36–38; Turner, "Conglomerate Mergers and Section 7 of the Clayton Act," p. 1332; Scherer, "Economies of Scale and Industrial Concentration," p. 43; Malcolm S. Salter and Wolf A. Weinhold, "Diversification via Acquisition: Creating Value," *Harvard Business Review,* vol. 56 (July-August 1978), pp. 166, 171–72, citing an example.

[129] Scherer, "Economies of Scale and Industrial Concentration," p. 42; Carleton, Harris, and Stewart, *An Empirical Study of Merger Motives,* p. 12; Senate Report 96–444, pp. 30, 159; "Conglomerate Mergers: A Study of Competition, Power, and Philosophy," p. C–9, citing Bork. Mergers, it is claimed, increase the flexibility of the conglomerate in responding to market opportunities, and such diversification may mesh distribution of products with different product life cycles, thus keeping sales and distribution staff continually busy. Weston, "Industrial Concentration, Mergers, and Growth: A Summary," p. 39. Markham claims that a conglomerate that operates in many markets can allocate more funds to R & D because it has more fronts on which it can apply R & D results than single-product firms of the same size; *Mergers and Economic Efficiency,* p. 10.

[130] Weston, "Industrial Concentration, Mergers, and Growth: A Summary," pp. 39, 44.

[131] Dennis C. Mueller, "The Effects of Conglomerate Mergers," *Journal of Banking and Finance,* vol. 1 (December 1977), p. 317; Scherer, "Economies of Scale and Industrial Concentration," pp. 41–42; *1979 S. 600 Hearings,* vol. 2, p. 318, statement of Birdzell. See also Peter Steiner, *Mergers: Motives, Effects, Policies* (Ann Arbor: University of Michigan Press, 1975), p. 79.

[132] *1979 S. 600 Hearings,* vol. 1, p. 173, statement of Dougherty. See also Oliver Williamson, *Markets and Hierarchies: Analysis and Antitrust Implications* (New York: The Free Press, 1975), pp. 155–75.

[133] *1979 S. 600 Hearings,* vol. 2, p. 100, statement of Robert S. Hatfield, chairman and chief executive officer of The Continental Group, Inc.

[134] Ibid.

[135] Weston, "Industrial Concentration, Mergers, and Growth: A Summary," pp. 33, 43; Weston, "Response to Reynolds' Review," p. 106; Markham, "Merger Policy under the New Section 7," pp. 489, 493–94; "Antitrust: Mergers, FTC Procedures, Class Actions Are Probed," *BNA DER,* August 7, 1980, pp. A–13,

A–14, statement of Professor Morris A. Adelman of Massachusetts Institute of Technology; and see F.T.C. v. Procter & Gamble Co., 386 U.S. 568, 598, 603, separate opinion of Justice Harlan.

[136] *1979 S. 600 Hearings,* vol. 2, p. 318, statement of Birdzell.

[137] *1978 Merger Hearings,* p. 211, statement of Shenefield; Steiner, *Mergers,* p. 78.

[138] *1978 Merger Hearings,* p. 211, statement of Shenefield, citing Robert L. Conn, "The Failing Firm/Industry Doctrines in Conglomerate Mergers," *The Journal of Industrial Economics,* vol. 24 (March 1976), pp. 181–87.

[139] *1979 S. 600 Hearings,* vol. 2, pp. 138–39, statement of Scherer; ibid., vol. 1, pp. 68–69, statement of Shenefield; Richard O. Levine, "Comments on Industrial Concentration, Mergers, and Growth," in *Mergers and Economic Efficiency,* pp. 45, 47; Larry Kramer, "Pertschuk Sees Danger in Recent Merger Trend," *Washington Post,* May 8, 1979, p. D–14, conglomerates involve mostly healthy firms; "Antitrust: SBA Official Calls for Legislation," *BNA DER,* February 8, 1980.

[140] *1978 Merger Hearings,* p. 181, statement of Adams.

[141] *1979 S. 600 Hearings,* vol. 2, p. 139, statement of Scherer; ibid., vol. 1, p. 174, statement of Dougherty.

[142] *1979 S. 600 Hearings,* vol. 1, p. 219, statement of Dougherty; ibid., p. 39, statement of Nader and Green.

[143] Ibid., vol. 1, p. 221, statement of Dougherty; see also Richard Cyert and James March, *A Behavioral Theory of the Firm* (Englewood Cliffs, N.J.: Prentice Hall, 1963); Harvey Leibenstein, *Beyond Economic Man: A New Foundation for Microeconomics* (Cambridge, Mass.: Harvard University Press, 1976).

[144] Walter Adams and Joel Dilram, "Big Steel, Invention, and Innovation," *Quarterly Journal of Economics,* vol. 80 (May 1966), pp. 167–89; Burton Klein, *Dynamic Economics* (Cambridge, Mass.: Harvard University Press, 1977), p. 189, cited in *1979 S. 600 Hearings,* vol. 1, p. 223, statement of Dougherty.

[145] *1979 S. 600 Hearings,* vol. 1, pp. 40–41, statement of Nader and Green, quoting Henry Simons; Green, *The Closed Enterprise System,* p. 27. See Carleton, Harris, and Stewart, *An Empirical Study of Merger Motives,* p. 24, for managerial objectives in mergers.

[146] F. M. Scherer, "The Posnerian Harvest: Separating the Wheat from the Chaff," *Yale Law Journal,* vol. 86 (April 1977), pp. 974, 988; and see Salter and Weinhold, "Diversification via Acquisition: Creating Value," p. 171.

[147] See, for example, *1979 S. 600 Hearings,* vol. 1, p. 67, statement of Shenefield; ibid., pp. 174–86, statement of Dougherty; ibid., pp. 303–5, statement of Mueller; ibid., pp. 139–42, statement of Scherer, who cites the empirical studies on which the proponents rely. The first group of studies sought to compare profitability patterns of companies prone to horizontal merger with the patterns of otherwise similar low-merger companies of the merger-prone industries. Scherer states that these studies suggest that the postmerger profitability experience of merger-prone companies was either less successful or not significantly more successful than that

of the others. Two similar studies looked directly at the profitability of businesses acquired by conglomerates. One of these two studies concluded that the profit/sales ratio of acquired firms did not vary significantly from that of a control group, and the other concluded that the ratio was lower by a statistically significant margin than the ratio for the control group. A third group of studies compared the overall profitability of a sample of conglomerates with the profitability of a control group. Scherer claims that, to the extent these studies fall into a coherent pattern, they suggest that the hyperactive conglomerates of the 1960s did well in their heyday by acquiring companies with strong profit histories and prospects. There is no indication, however, that they did any better with assets they acquired than the acquired companies would have done if they had remained independent. After problems developed in the late 1960s, the overall profitability of the conglomerates may well have been lower than it would have been for the sum of their independent parts. A fourth group of studies compared the return on a portfolio of securities of merger-intensive firms with the return of a comparable portfolio of firms emphasizing internal growth. Most of the studies concluded that the former performed no better than, and often worse than, the latter. The samples employed in these studies, however, have been sharply criticized.

[148] Carleton, Harris, and Stewart, *An Empirical Study of Merger Motives,* pp. 11–12.

[149] Robert J. Reynolds, "A Review of 'Industrial Concentration, Mergers, and Growth,' " in *Mergers and Economic Efficiency,* p. 76; Siegfried, *The Economics of Firm Size, Market Structure, and Social Performance,* p. 77, comments of Professor Harvey S. Goldschmid of Columbia Law School.

[150] Levine, "Comments on Industrial Concentration, Mergers, and Growth," p. 46.

[151] *1979 S. 600 Hearings,* vol. 2, p. 25, statement of Baxter; Brozen, "A Comment on Weston's Industrial Concentration, Mergers, and Growth," pp. 64–68.

[152] The studies that support the opponents' position are set forth in *1979 S. 600 Hearings,* vol. 2, pp. 16–17, statement of Posner. The first group of studies suggests that the acquired firm's shareholders receive large premiums at the time of merger. Many of the same studies also suggest that the acquiring firm's shareholders receive small gain, if any, from the merger. Other studies suggest that the comparative profitability of conglomerates is ambiguous, but that in any event the gains or losses after merger are not large and the returns are competitive. One study concludes that acquired firms are not efficiently managed.

[153] Weston, "Response to Reynolds' Review," pp. 83, 87; Weston, "Industrial Concentration, Mergers, and Growth: A Summary," p. 41; Benston, *Conglomerate Mergers: Causes, Consequences, and Remedies,* pp. 45–49.

[154] Weston, "Industrial Concentration, Mergers, and Growth: A Summary," pp. 42–43; *Mergers and Economic Efficiency,* p. 8, comments of Jerry J. Jasinowski, assistant secretary of commerce for policy; Turner, "Conglomerate Mergers and Section 7 of the Clayton Act," p. 1316; Brozen, "A Comment on Weston's Industrial Concentration, Mergers, and Growth," p. 69.

[155] Shapiro, "The Antitrust Syndrome: Is Bigness Bad?" p. 563; "Conglomerate Mergers: A Study of Competition, Power, and Philosophy," p. C–10, quoting Bork; Weston, "Response to Reynolds' Review," pp. 80, 86.

[156] *1978 Merger Hearings,* pp. 132, 137, 138, statement of Howard M. Wachtel, professor of economics, American University.

[157] *1979 S. 600 Hearings,* vol. 1, pp. 474–75, statement of Phillip Cagan, professor of economics, Columbia University. For a discussion of the "administered pricing" concept advanced by Gardiner Means in congressional testimony in 1935 and in 1958, as well as for citation of studies concluding that concentration in particular industries is not a cause of inflation, see Demsetz, *The Market Concentration Doctrine,* pp. 4–10; J. Fred Weston and Steven H. Lustgarten, "Concentration and Wage-Price Changes," in Goldschmid, Mann, and Weston, *Industrial Concentration: The New Learning,* pp. 307–32; Weston, "Response to Reynolds' Review," p. 80; Steven H. Lustgarten, *Industrial Concentration and Inflation* (Washington, D.C.: American Enterprise Institute, 1975). Proponents argue that inflation from administered pricing occurs in all industries, whether concentrated or not. Abba Lerner, professor of economics at the City University of New York, cites the problem of administered pricing, which he refers to as "sellers' inflation," but he does not believe that a more vigorous antimonopoly program would be more than temporarily effective against sellers' inflation. Lerner, "Monopoly Power: Causes of Inflation at Less Than Full Employment," pp. 197, 200–201.

[158] Dam, "The 'Big Is Bad' Bill."

[159] *1979 S. 600 Hearings,* vol. 1, pp. 367–68, statement of then Senator Adlai E. Stevenson III (D-Ill.).

[160] Ibid., p. 430, statement of Markham.

[161] "Should There Be A Ban on Big Company Mergers?" p. 8.

[162] "New Thrust in Antitrust," *Time,* May 21, 1979, pp. 62, 64, quoting Shapiro; Boucher, *The Process of Conglomerate Mergers,* pp. 138, 144.

[163] *1979 S. 600 Hearings,* vol. 2, p. 40, statement of Baker; ibid., vol. 1, p. 370, statement of Senator Stevenson.

[164] Ibid., vol. 2, pp. 40–41, statement of Baker; ibid., vol. 1, p. 419, statement of Kenneth W. Dam, professor of international legal studies, University of Chicago Law School; Shapiro, "The Antitrust Syndrome: Is Bigness Bad?" p. 563; "New Thrust in Antitrust," p. 64, citing Shapiro; Dam, "The 'Big Is Bad' Bill"; Boucher, *The Process of Conglomerate Mergers,* p. 145.

[165] "Antitrust: SBA Official Calls for Legislation to Curb Merger Growth by Conglomerates," *BNA DER,* February 8, 1980, pp. A–12, A–13; see Senate Report 96–444, p. 68.

[166] *1979 S. 600 Hearings,* vol. 1, pp. 138–40, statement of Dougherty, citing Richard Hofstadter, *The Age of Reform* (New York: Knopf, 1955), pp. 241, 277.

[167] Brown Shoe Co. v. United States, 370 U.S. 294, 316 (1962).

[168] United States v. Aluminum Co. of America, 148 F. 2d 416, 428 (2d Cir. 1945).

[169] "New Thrust in Antitrust," p. 63; Edwin M. Epstein, "Firm Size and Structure, Market Power and Business Political Influence: A Review of the Literature," in Siegfried, *The Economics of Firm Size, Market Structure, and Social Performance,* p. 240, and comments of Goldschmid at p. 73.

[170] See Continental T.V., Inc. v. GTE Sylvania, Inc., 443 U.S. 36 (1977); National Society of Professional Engineers v. United States, 435 U.S. 679 (1978), discussed in Siegfried, *The Economics of Firm Size, Market Structure, and Social Performance,* p. 11; Turner, "Conglomerate Mergers and Section 7 of the Clayton Act," pp. 1325, 1395.

[171] *1979 S. 600 Hearings,* vol. 2, p. 49, statement of Ira M. Millstein, former chairman of the American Bar Association's Antitrust Law Section; "Conglomerate Mergers: A Study of Competition, Power, and Philosophy," p. C–22. Senator Hatch argues: "Throughout our history, 'we the people' have placed primary reliance on unfettered competition. There is no viable justification to now replace market forces with a government-imposed prohibition based on size." See "Should There Be a Ban on Big Company Mergers?" p. 8.

[172] *1979 S. 600 Hearings,* vol. 2, p. 10, statement of Posner; ibid., pp. 99–100, statement of Hatfield.

[173] Ibid., vol. 1, p. 18, statement of William S. Comanor, former director, Bureau of Economics, Federal Trade Commission.

[174] Phillip Areeda and Donald Turner, *Antitrust Law,* vol. 1 (Boston: Little, Brown, & Co., 1978), p. 22. Areeda and Turner do not share this view.

[175] *1979 S. 600 Hearings,* vol. 1, pp. 17–18, statement of Comanor; William S. Comanor, "Conglomerate Mergers: Considerations of Public Policy," in *Mergers and Economic Efficiency,* pp. 56–58, 61.

[176] Shapiro, "The Antitrust Syndrome: Is Bigness Bad?" p. 563.

[177] *1979 S. 600 Hearings,* vol. 1, p. 430, statement of Markham.

[178] Bork, *The Antitrust Paradox,* p. 54.

[179] Bain, *Industrial Organization,* p. 91.

[180] Adams, "Corporate Power and Economic Apologetics," p. 368.

[181] Kramer, "Pertschuk Sees Danger in Recent Merger Trend," p. D–14; *1979 S. 600 Hearings,* vol. 1, p. 40, statement of Nader and Green; ibid., p. 193, statement of Dougherty citing Charles Lindblom, *Politics and Markets: The World's Political Economic Systems* (New York: Basic Books, 1977), p. 165.

[182] *1979 S. 600 Hearings,* vol. 1, p. 430, statement of Markham; ibid., p. 189, statement of Dougherty citing Edwin Epstein, *The Corporation in American Politics* (Englewood Cliffs, N.J.: Prentice-Hall, 1969), p. 224.

[183] *1979 S. 600 Hearings,* vol. 2, p. 84, statement of Gordon Tullock, director, Center for Studies of Public Choice, Virginia Polytechnic Institute and State University.

[184] Robert Pitofsky, "The Political Content of Antitrust," in *Antitrust Law and Economics* (Houston: Dame Publications, 1980), p. 169, cited in *1979 S. 600 Hearings,* vol. 1, p. 190, statement of Dougherty.

[185] *1978 Merger Hearings,* p. 156, statement of Pertschuk.

[186] Lester Salamon and John Siegfried, "Economic Power and Political Influence: The Impact of Industry Structure on Public Policy," *American Political Science Review,* vol. 71 (September 1977), pp. 1028–29, cited in *1979 S. 600 Hearings,* vol. 1, pp. 195–97, statement of Dougherty; H. Michael Mann and Karen McCormick, "Firm Attributes and the Propensity to Influence the Political System," in Siegfried, *The Economics of Firm Size, Market Structure, and Social Performance,* p. 301.

[187] Ralph Nader and Mark Green, *Taming the Giant Corporation* (New York: Norton, 1976), pp. 153–54; National Industrial Conference Board, "The Role of Business in Public Affairs," *Studies in Public Affairs,* vol. 2 (1978), p. 8; Raymond A. Bauer, Ithiel de Sola Pool, and Lewis Anthony Dexter, *American Business and Public Policy* (New York: Atherton Press, 1963), p. 227, cited in *1979 S. 600 Hearings,* vol. 1, pp. 198–201, statement of Dougherty.

[188] Nader and Green, *Taming the Giant Corporation,* p. 223. Representative Henry S. Reuss (D-Wis.) asks: "What happens when a nationwide conglomerate acquires outlets in 218 congressional districts and thus obtains a headlock on the majority of the House?" "Conglomerate Mergers: A Study of Competition, Power, and Philosophy," p. C–24.

[189] *Mergers and Economic Efficiency,* p. 24.

[190] *New York Times,* January 18, 1979, p. A–19, cited in *1979 S. 600 Hearings,* vol. 1, p. 198, statement of Dougherty.

[191] Edwin Epstein, "Business and Labor in the American Electoral Process—A Policy Analysis of Federal Regulation—The Rise of Political Action Committees," Institute of Government Studies, University of California, Berkeley, Working Papers (1979), pp. 31–32, cited in *1979 S. 600 Hearings,* vol. 1, pp. 198–99, statement of Dougherty.

[192] See Siegfried, *The Economics of Firm Size, Market Structure, and Social Performance,* p. 304.

[193] *1979 S. 600 Hearings,* vol. 2, p. 64, statement of Edwin M. Epstein, professor, School of Business Administration, University of California, Berkeley.

[194] Ibid., p. 11, statement of Posner.

[195] Ibid., p. 84, statement of Tullock.

[196] Ibid., p. 11, statement of Posner.

[197] Ibid., pp. 84–85, statement of Tullock.

[198] Epstein, "Firm Size and Structure, Market Power and Business Political Influence," p. 241; Mann and McCormick, "Firm Attributes and the Propensity to Influence the Political System," p. 311; Cathleen Coolidge and Gordon Tullock, "Firm Size and Political Power," in Siegfried, *The Economics of Firm Size, Market Structure, and Social Performance,* p. 48.

[199] Federal Election Commission Interim Report No. 2, "Party and Non-Party Political Organizations, Non-Party Political Committees" (September 1978), cited in *1979 S. 600 Hearings,* vol. 2, pp. 67–69, statement of Edwin M. Epstein; see also Epstein, "Firm Size and Structure, Market Power and Business Political Influence," p. 278.

[200] *1979 S. 600 Hearings,* vol. 1, p. 65, statement of Shenefield.

[201] Speech delivered at American Bar Association meeting in New York, New York (August 7, 1978); *1979 S. 600 Hearings,* vol. 1, p. 64, statement of Shenefield; *1978 Merger Hearings,* p. 260, statement of Burck.

[202] See *1979 S. 600 Hearings,* vol. 2, p. 80, note 1, statement of Tullock, for background on the statement and a list of those who have cited it with approval.

[203] Ibid., pp. 80–81.

[204] Ibid.

[205] Ibid., p. 151, statement of Brodley.

[206] Ibid., vol. 1, p. 203, statement of Dougherty.

[207] Ibid., vol. 1, pp. 205–7, statement of Dougherty citing Lindblom, *Politics and Markets,* pp. 154–55; ibid., vol. 2, pp. 151–52, statement of Brodley.

[208] Ibid., vol. 1, pp. 203, 208–9, statement of Dougherty. Maintenance of a multitude of decision centers is thus the primary social objective of proponents of conglomerate legislation. "Conglomerate Mergers: A Study of Competition, Power, and Philosophy," p. C–21, quoting Pertschuk; Donald J. Dewey, "The New Learning: One Man's View," in Goldschmid, Mann, and Weston, *Industrial Concentration: The New Learning,* pp. 1, 13.

[209] *1979 S. 600 Hearings,* vol. 2, pp. 51–52, statement of Millstein.

[210] Ibid., vol. 2, p. 70, statement of Epstein citing Royal Commission on Corporate Concentration, "Corporate Social Performance in Canada," Study No. 21, A Background Report Prepared by the Niagara Institute (1977).

[211] *Mergers and Economic Efficiency,* p. 9; and see Milton Friedman, "Monopoly and the Social Responsibility of Business and Labor," pp. 57, 66. Oliver E. Williamson, professor of economics at the University of Pennsylvania, maintains that, if firms are diverted from their principal purpose to pursue a variety of social goals for which they have no comparative advantage, their efficiency features are likely to be sacrificed and the realization of these other social purposes is unlikely to be well served. Siegfried, *The Economics of Firm Size, Market Structure, and Social Performance,* p. 79.

[212] Benston, *Conglomerate Mergers: Causes, Consequences, and Remedies,* p. 53. Bork would make *consumer* welfare the touchstone of antitrust enforcement, and he regards other goals as inappropriate. Bork, *The Antitrust Paradox,* p. 56.

[213] *1978 Merger Hearings,* p. 141, statement of Charles Craypo, associate professor of labor studies, Pennsylvania State University; Robert N. Stern and Howard Aldrich, "The Effect of Absentee Firm Control on Local Community Welfare: A

Survey," in Siegfried, *The Economics of Firm Size, Market Structure, and Social Performance,* pp. 162, 163, 167, 169; Siegfried, *The Economics of Firm Size, Market Structure, and Social Performance,* p. 228, comments of Willard F. Mueller. House Report 96–1447, p. 7, quoting Professor David Stern; *1979 S. 600 Hearings,* vol. 1, p. 64, statement of Shenefield.

[214] Justice Douglas, quoted in *1979 S. 600 Hearings,* vol. 1, p. 40, statement of Nader and Green. See also *1978 Merger Hearings,* p. 258, statement of Burck.

[215] *1979 S. 600 Hearings,* vol. 2, p. 11, statement of Posner.

[216] Ibid., pp. 69–70, statement of Epstein; Siegfried, *The Economics of Firm Size, Market Structure, and Social Performance,* p. 233, comment of Ivar Berg, professor of sociology, University of Pennsylvania.

[217] Shapiro, "The Antitrust Syndrome: Is Bigness Bad?" p. 564.

[218] *1979 S. 600 Hearings,* vol. 1, pp. 64–65, statement of Shenefield.

[219] Ibid., vol. 2, p. 24, statement of Baxter.

[220] Benston, *Conglomerate Mergers: Causes, Consequences, and Remedies,* pp. 53–54; "Conglomerate Mergers: A Study of Competition, Power, and Philosophy," p. C–26.

[221] Shapiro, "The Antitrust Syndrome: Is Bigness Bad?" p. 564.

[222] *1979 S. 600 Hearings,* vol. 2, p. 11, statement of Posner; "Conglomerate Mergers: A Study of Competition, Power, and Philosophy," p. C–26.

[223] Stern and Aldrich, "The Effect of Absentee Firm Control on Local Community Welfare," pp. 162, 167–68; House Report 96–1447, p. 13; *1978 Merger Hearings,* p. 141, statement of Craypo; and see "Conglomerate Mergers: A Study of Competition, Power, and Philosophy," p. C–21, quoting Pertschuk that "the growth of institutions beyond human scale can cause alienation, resulting in inefficiency and unhappiness."

[224] Siegfried, *The Economics of Firm Size, Market Structure, and Social Performance,* p. 233, comments of Berg.

[225] Benston, *Conglomerate Mergers: Causes, Consequences, and Remedies,* p. 53; and see "Conglomerate Mergers: A Study of Competition, Power, and Philosophy," p. C–25.

[226] *1979 S. 600 Hearings,* vol. 2, pp. 41–42, statement of Baker.

[227] Ibid., p. 43, statement of Baker; Benston, *Conglomerate Mergers: Causes, Consequences, and Remedies,* pp. 67–68.

[228] *1979 S. 600 Hearings,* vol. 2, p. 26, statement of Baxter.

[229] McCracken and Moore, *Competition and Market Concentration in the American Economy,* pp. 8–9; Sims, "Report of the President's Commission on Antitrust," p. 32; Weston, "Industrial Concentration, Mergers, and Growth: A Summary," p. 44. John S. McGee, professor of economics at the University of Washington, Seattle, claims such industrial reorganization schemes have much the same effect

as dictating to consumers what and from whom they may buy, and these are both uneconomic and tyrannical. Goldschmid, Mann, and Weston, *Industrial Concentration: The New Learning,* p. 104.

[230] *1979 S. 600 Hearings,* vol. 2, p. 27, statement of Baxter.

[231] See Senate Report 96–444, p. 240, additional views of Senator Hatch who regards shifting the burden of proof to defendants as a radical and unjust change at odds with the most basic principles of American jurisprudence.

[232] *1979 S. 600 Hearings,* vol. 2, p. 42, statement of Baker.

[233] Weston, "Industrial Concentration, Mergers, and Growth: A Summary," p. 41; Richard A. Posner, "Problems of a Policy of Deconcentration," in Goldschmid, Mann, and Weston, *Industrial Concentration: The New Learning,* pp. 393, 397; Weiss, "The Concentration-Profits Relationship and Antitrust," p. 233.

[234] Boucher, *The Process of Conglomerate Mergers,* p. 147.

[235] Levine, "Comments on Industrial Concentration, Mergers and Growth," p. 50.